Blind Ambition

Blind Ambition

The Remarkable Story of a 4-time
World Disabled Water-Ski Champion

**Janet Gray
with Lorraine Wylie**

Gill & Macmillan

Gill & Macmillan Ltd
Hume Avenue, Park West, Dublin 12
with associated companies throughout the world
www.gillmacmillan.ie

Typography design by Make Communication
Print origination by Síofra Murphy
Printed by ColourBooks Ltd, Dublin

This book is typeset in Linotype Minion and Neue Helvetica.

The paper used in this book comes from the wood pulp of
managed forests. For every tree felled, at least one tree is
planted, thereby renewing natural resources.

A CIP catalogue record for this book is available
from the British Library.

5 4 3 2 1

Contents

FOREWORD BY EAMONN HOLMES   VII

ACKNOWLEDGMENTS   IX

1.	The Early Years	1
2.	Darkness Encroaches	11
3.	The Thirty-Nine Steps	21
4.	Married Life	30
5.	A New Beginning	40
6.	Competition Fever	50
7.	Aiming High	58
8.	Eastern Delight	67
9.	World Champion	77
10.	The Millennium	85
11.	Down Under	94
12.	Hooked on a Feeling	104
13.	The Accident	115
14.	Oblivion	125
15.	Home Again	135
16.	Life in the Royal Victoria Hospital	145
17.	Hell on Wheels	154
18.	The Return to Florida	163
19.	The Ultimate Buzz	171
20.	Living the Dream	181
21.	Moving On	191
22.	The Fire	200

EPILOGUE   211

Foreword

Breaking boundaries and breaking bones just about sums up the Janet I know. When they made Janet Gray, they broke the mould. Well they probably didn't—she probably did, at about 60 mph on the top of some lake! The woman never knows when she is beaten—and so far she never has been. Not only is Janet an exceptional athlete, she's an exceptional person. Meeting and interviewing her over the years has always been an inspiring and very humbling experience. Humbling because very quickly you realise how special Janet is. There's almost an aura shining from her—an aura of energy, positivity and kindness. In theory, because she is blind, Janet's world should be dark. In practice it just can't be—she simply wouldn't allow it.

Janet Gray's story is not about sport or handicap, it's about living and enjoying what life has to offer whatever the circumstances. Being in Janet's company is a good feeling. Hearing about her battles against adversity, records, barriers and injury is, although almost unbelievable at times, inspiring.

I like the woman very much, but her husband Paul loves her. He would have to. He not only supports her, he encourages her in all that she does. If I hadn't met Paul, I suspect I would have always harboured the suspicion that Janet is slightly bonkers—but the law of probability dictates that it's unlikely the two of them together are equally bonkers! They make a great team and a great story. So enjoy the read and enjoy the journey Janet will bring you on. The highs and lows, the sadness, the ecstasy, the pain and poignancy and lots and lots of cold water. It's all here and together it's what makes Janet Gray the person she is—a person who has my total respect and admiration.

Eamonn Holmes

Acknowledgments

There are many people who have featured greatly in my life and, while it is impossible to name them all, I am nevertheless grateful for their help. From my earliest days, I have been surrounded by those who have shown me that unconditial love so peculiar to a close family unit. While Mum, Pop and Ian have occupied the chief roles, I cannot ignore the wonderful contribution of my extended family at home and abroad.

I would also like to take this opportunity to thank the medical experts at the Royal Victoria Hospital who, during my teenage years, battled so hard to save my sight.

Thanks must also go to everyone associated with helping me regain independence and normality as I struggled to come to terms with blindness.

My entry into water-skiing introduced me not only to a fantastic sport but a wonderful set of people and I'd like to extend my sincere appreciation for their professional expertise and friendship. It would be impossible to speak of my career without mentioning some of the people who sponsored and encouraged me along the way. With this in mind, I pay tribute to Sport Northern Ireland, Connelly Skis Inc., Copper Hairdressing Salon and all those who have supported me.

The year 2004 brought devastation to my life but it also brought an immense wealth of expertise and knowledge. I can never repay the debt I owe Dr David Halpern and his medical team at Tampa General Hospital for everything they have done. Likewise, I owe an enormous debt to staff at the Royal Victoria Hospital as well as Dr Philip Glasgow and his team at the Sports Institute Northern Ireland. I'd also like to pay tribute to my friend Dame Mary Peters.

To all those whom I have omitted to mention, particularly my chums in the media, you remain in my thoughts.

My sincerest thanks must also go to Eamonn Holmes and my friend and co-writer, Lorraine Wylie.

Finally, I'd like to offer both thanks and love to the man who has stood by me, whatever life has thrown—my husband, Paul: I love you.

Chapter 1
The Early Years

The sixties opened with a journey to the bottom of the sea and ended with a visit to the moon. Sandwiched between Jacques Piccard's record-breaking descent to the bottom of the Pacific Ocean and Neil Armstrong's dramatic lunar steps, a cultural revolution shaped and changed everything from fashion to politics. Characterised by innovation and invention, there's no doubt that the sixties was an exciting time to be born.

My arrival on 16 August 1962 at Belfast's Jubilee Maternity Hospital may have made little impact on the world at large, but for my parents, Maureen and John Snowdon, the event proved the highlight of their year. Mum, delighted with the baby daughter they had named Janet, decided to give up her job as a legal secretary and stay at home to look after me. Pop, a service engineer for Creda, continued to travel all over the Province, providing for his young family. At the end of a long day, he loved nothing better than returning home to Dundonald, at that time still little more than a village, to cuddle and play with his equally delighted daughter. Over the next couple of years, life settled into a pattern of contented domesticity. The birth of my brother Ian added yet another splash of joy to my parents' world and provided an adored playmate for me. There was no sign of the cruel blows fate had in store for the Snowdon family.

The ability to see the world in all its Technicolor glory is something most of us take for granted. As a child, the familiar sight of Mum's face, Dad's infectious grin or my little brother's cherubic features were just a normal part of life. I had no idea such treasures could be snatched away, forever hidden behind a curtain of inky blackness. Looking back, my childhood appears to have been painted in some of nature's most vivid shades—from the little white doll's pram with its scarlet hood and motif to the bright red fire engines that proved such a thrill when Granda Brown treated me to a visit at the local station. Later, a trip to Dublin's Phoenix Park lent vibrant tones of rich brown earth, emerald green grass and denim blue skies. As well as colour, my young eyes were introduced to some of the shapes and sizes within the animal kingdom. Forty years later, I can still recall the grey, wrinkled skin of a baby elephant who came to say hello to his four-year-old visitor and the tiny foal whose injured hoof completely reduced me to tears. Although I didn't realise it at the time, those early images of life would eventually provide not only a sense of form, but a kaleidoscope of colour to penetrate a world of utter darkness.

My first encounter with blindness was via a second-hand route. The devastation of losing one of the body's major senses could not be grasped by childish logic or comprehension. However, for my parents, Pop's sudden catapult into perpetual night was excruciatingly painful. Diagnosed with myopia as a young man, Pop had always worn glasses. But when his sight began to deteriorate at an alarming rate, doctors referred him to specialists at the Moorfields Eye Hospital in London. After a diagnosis of an extremely rare form of glaucoma, he underwent several gruelling operations in a bid to save his sight. Sadly, by the time he returned to Northern Ireland, Pop had to acknowledge the fact that he would never see again. As well as worrying about her husband's physical and psychological well-being, Mum struggled with the financial impact of the situation. Unable to see, Pop rapidly lost his driving licence and was no longer able to work or contribute to the family budget. With no income, a mortgage to pay and mouths to feed, my poor mum endured many sleepless nights. Yet, despite the circumstances, she managed to shield us from everything and provide the support her husband so desperately needed.

Eventually, in early 1966, Pop decided to learn the skills that would help him function in his new and frightening world. After completing a course designed to teach mobility, the use of a white cane and general coping mechanisms for daily life, Pop returned from Torquay's Manor House Rehabilitation Centre for the Blind and immediately embarked on another training scheme to learn the rudiments of engineering. The latter was based at Feldon House in Whiteabbey and was to lead to a new job with Standard Telephones and Cables.

Gradually, as Pop managed to overcome his visual challenge, life regained a semblance of normality. Any fears that this dangerous form of glaucoma may strike the next generation of Snowdon children were quickly and confidently put to rest. Doctors assured my parents that, although tragic, Pop's condition was nothing more than an unfortunate but isolated incident.

However, when my little brother's vision began to follow a similar pattern, my parents nursed an aching premonition of what lay ahead.

Initially, Ian's prognosis seemed much less traumatic. Granted, according to Mr Cowan, Pop's eye specialist, the youngster had indeed developed the same type of glaucoma. Nevertheless, medical experts offered a branch of hope. With medical treatment that involved daily applications of eye drops, the condition could be monitored and kept under control. Ian needn't inhabit the same sightless world as his dad. During this time, our parents decided that, despite natural inclinations, they would resist the temptation to wrap Ian in cotton wool and avoid depriving him of a normal childhood. Naturally, there had to be some basic ground rules, such as restricting Ian's exuberant inclination for a bit of boyish rough and tumble. Even the slightest bump on his head could exaggerate the problem. Nevertheless, despite their best efforts, endless eye drops and numerous painful operations, my twelve-year-old brother lost his sight.

By this stage, I was no longer protected by childish ignorance. Pop's descent into blindness may not have penetrated my horizons of innocent awareness but Ian's journey towards a sightless future was terrifyingly real. I cannot describe my heartache as I watched my lovely brother succumb to his hereditary fate. But I can't in all honesty paint a picture of morbid dread or mournful foreboding. Ian, like our parents, enjoys a fantastic sense of fun and zest for life. I seem to recall that, on several occasions, he attempted to avoid dish-washing duty on the premise that, as he would soon lose his ability to see his favourite television programmes, it was necessary to view as many as possible. Despite the bittersweet irony of the situation, Mum and Dad remained pragmatic and quickly chased him into the kitchen!

As yet another member of the Snowdon family fell foul of the random gene, doctors were forced to revise their diagnosis. On this occasion, their considered opinion, although too late for Ian, offered me a ray of hope. Apparently, this particular form of glaucoma was confined to the male lineage and, thankfully, I would be spared. Poor Pop and Ian. Still, I couldn't help but hug myself with delight at such seeming good fortune. Future generations of

Snowdon women would live their lives in sharp and glorious focus.

While medical opinion was certain I had escaped catastrophe, doctors decided it would be a good idea to keep a check on my overall eyesight. It was during one such test they discovered I suffered from the same myopic condition that had plagued Pop's youth. The prescribed glasses for a self-conscious teenager were a nightmare. At every opportunity, I ditched the dreaded specs and opted for a squinty-eyed but much more glamorous view of the world.

Apart from a huge amount of energy, my early life was characterised by a fascination for water. Whether in puddles or ponds, I was determined to make a splash. Gran Brown, fearful that her granddaughter would end up way out of her depth, decided to invest in a course of swimming lessons and inadvertently ignited a series of events that would eventually lead to some of my greatest triumphs as well as my severest trials. By the time adolescence arrived, I was already an accomplished swimmer and looking forward to achieving the Open Water Certificate for life-saving skills. The day arrived, and together with the other potential rescuers, I took my place and prepared to swim into the icy waters at Helen's Bay. With temperatures hovering around six degrees it was a mind-numbing as well as toe-numbing experience. Fixing my eyes on the position of my friend Rosemary, who played the role of 'victim', I discarded my glasses and plunged into the freezing sea. Other myopic contestants also removed their spectacles and, for once, our ability was tested on swimming strengths instead of sight. Afterwards, with certificates duly earned, we huddled around a paraffin heater, hands clasping cups of hot soup, teeth chattering, and enjoyed the camaraderie that comes solely from the equality of success and achievement. Perhaps, in that moment, I found an area of life where the playing field was even and open to everyone, regardless of sensory challenges.

After a happy primary education, I joined the ranks at Graymount Girls' Secondary School. Set in beautiful grounds overlooking Belfast Lough, the school not only enjoyed a reputation for its ability to provide a range of skills tailored to individual ability, but also a romantic heritage certain to capture the imagination of any teenage girl. According to historic tales, Lord Gray (no relation) murdered his wife and hid her body in one of the mansion's upper rooms. Yet justice was seen to be done when, a few years later, a tile fell from the roof of his wife's secluded chamber and decapitated the unrepentant husband. Many times, my friends and I wandered the corridors in hushed but excited anticipation of witnessing an appearance from the famous 'Headless Horseman'. Unfortunately, he never bothered to feed our adolescent desire for romantic gore.

While haunting may not have been a subject approved for study, music was very definitely on the school curriculum. I couldn't sing a recognisable note but nevertheless, I knew a get out clause when I saw one. With interests that centred on after school activities like swimming or the church youth club, I tended to avoid anything that demanded any form of serious study. My decision to join the Wednesday afternoon school choir was based entirely on the number of classes I could possibly avoid. Sadly, the plan backfired when practice was moved to an after school slot. My years at Graymount are among some of my happiest memories. One of the major highlights was when our school was among ten invited to help mark the opening of the Mary Peters Track. After winning a gold medal in the pentathlon event at the 1972 Munich Olympics, Mary had raised a lot of money to provide the young people of Northern Ireland with athletic facilities. At the time, the Province was experiencing some of the worst of its troubled history and Mary's success helped boost morale, especially among the younger generation. Pupils from each school lined up to spell out a letter from

Mary's name, then, in perfect formation, paraded around the track. Our school, Graymount, formed the first 'E' in Peters. For those spectators sitting high up in the banks, or anyone with an aerial view, it must have been an impressive sight. As an ex-teacher at Graymount, Mary noticed and came over to speak to some of us from the school. I was so overwhelmed that an Olympic gold medal winner should talk to me, I was almost speechless! I'd no idea that one day we would become such great friends.

While my school career was packed with fun, with hindsight I can also trace the early signs that I would eventually join Pop and Ian in never-ending night.

The first event to set alarm bells ringing occurred during a routine check-up with my specialist. I hadn't noticed any significant difference in my vision so when Mr Cowan announced that I had to start using eye drops, a knot of fear formed in my stomach. The fact that the prescription was the same one Ian had used didn't help matters. Sensing my panic, Mr Cowan did his best to reassure me that the drops, designed to control eye pressure, were merely a pre-cautionary treatment. Still, in my heart, I think I knew something was terribly wrong. With 'O' level exams looming the last thing I needed was extra stress. Apart from emphasising the importance of daily applications, my parents didn't say much about the consultant's decision and within a few weeks, I decided to look on the bright side and hope for the best.

Six months later, at my next hospital appointment, Mr Cowan had worse news. Apparently the drops had failed to do the trick and I now needed an operation to lower the pressure. Once again, I seemed to be following the same path destiny had paved for my brother. It wasn't a direction I wanted to go as I knew only too well where it might lead. I can only imagine the turmoil and sense of 'déjà vu' my parents must have experienced. Nevertheless, within a month, while Mum was away on business, Pop, Grannie Snowdon and I made our way to Ward 28 in Belfast's Royal Victoria Hospital where surgeons hoped that, by making new drainage channels, eye pressure would decrease and damage to the optic nerve could be prevented. On this occasion, only one eye was to be operated on but, for a frightened teenager, the fact offered cold comfort. Although the surgery went extremely well, I can still recall the discomfort of having to lie flat on my back for a full week! Today, the procedure is much less complicated and can be carried out quickly and painlessly with the aid of laser. My left eye eventually underwent the same process but on this occasion, lying flat for seven days was a little less boring. Poor Ian once again had to have the same operation and was admitted to the room next to mine where, during the dreaded recovery phase, we passed the time shouting and joking to each other. Pop came up with a great way to help us communicate more easily. No doubt the walkie-talkie sets he brought us also helped make the ward a much quieter place.

Despite missing a lot of school, I was jubilant! Finally, I no longer had to wear the awful specs. My first pair of contact lenses boosted morale and my confidence soared, especially in front of boys! I was ready to get back to normality, study for exams and get on with what promised to be an exciting future. My headmistress had other ideas. Concerned that I would not be able to catch up, she told my parents that she had decided to withdraw my name from the 'O' level list. Needless to say, Pop and Mum were furious. There was no way they would allow anyone to deny their daughter her rights. Threatening to lodge a complaint with both the school's Board of Governors and the Education Authority, Mum insisted I was given the same opportunity as any other student.

Admittedly, catching up on missed work was a hard slog. But I was determined to succeed and spent every spare moment making up for lost time. However, the next visit to Mr Cowan's clinic added an unwelcome as well as unexpected incentive. Apparently, despite the operation's initial success, my vision was rapidly deteriorating. To my shock and horror, my specialist advised my parents it would be best if I left Graymount and joined Ian at the Jordanstown School for the Blind. I was sixteen years old; I didn't want to leave my friends. I didn't want to change schools and more importantly, I didn't want to be different. With characteristic stubbornness, I refused to give in and insisted I would continue my education at Graymount. Looking back, I realise that it was during this time that I began to train myself to rely on my memory instead of sight. In fact, I came up with some pretty ingenious ways to disguise my failing vision. When the school nurse arrived to carry out routine eye tests, I realised that if I could achieve a decent result, the other girls wouldn't view me as different and everyone would accept that there was no need for me to attend a school for the blind. While I could read the first five lines of the Snellen chart, the remainder was beyond me. Fortunately, my surname placed me halfway down the queue of students and I decided to use the fact to my advantage. Waiting for my turn, I listened intently to the others rhyme off the letters so that by the time the nurse asked me to read, I knew them all by heart!

To everyone's amazement and delight, I not only entered all my 'O' level exams but achieved predominantly A grades. With such good results, my ambition grew and I decided to remain at school and study for 'A' levels. By the time I was seventeen, I had another goal in mind. This time, I was after some real independence and wanted to learn to drive. My vision was still within legal limits so my parents decided to give me driving lessons as a birthday present. I was ecstatic. I thoroughly enjoyed the weekly lessons with my instructor but I loved nothing more than the practice sessions with

Granda Billy, Mum's dad. Granda, never stressed or agitated, instilled confidence in his young pupil. He also managed to pass on his passion for cars and before long I could memorise and recount makes, models and registration marks of all his vehicles. Granda's patience combined with the instructor's expertise paid off and the day I passed my driving test was definitely among my happiest.

Advanced level study required a lot more work than first anticipated. The intense and long periods of study began taking their toll, leaving my eyes feeling tired and strained. Yet, I was determined not to quit. Then, just as life seemed to swing in my favour, a nasty throat infection and a routine visit to our GP launched me on a downward spiral. Although I had been prescribed the same medication as my brother and underwent identical surgery, no-one had ever suggested I shared his condition. I simply assumed that I suffered from myopia and that surgery had prevented any serious damage. However, as I sat in my GP's office, waiting for him to write a prescription to soothe my aching throat, I was totally unprepared for the diagnosis he was about to deliver. Glancing at my notes, the doctor suddenly announced that, as I suffered from glaucoma, he would have to alter his original choice of treatment. I was stunned. When I eventually found my voice and asked if it was the same strain that had robbed Pop and Ian of sight, the doctor, pressed for time and unaware of my terror, completely destroyed my world with a casual nod of assent.

Unbelievably, my worst fears had been confirmed. Glaucoma had finally scored a hat trick in the Snowdon household.

Chapter 2
Darkness Encroaches

Initially, the revelation that I suffered from the same condition as Pop and Ian launched me into a state of unbelievable panic. The possibility that I too could be catapulted into a world of darkness haunted my dreams and dominated every waking moment. Barely out of my teens, such a prospect proved too dreadful to contemplate. In a bid to cope, or perhaps deny reality, I hugged the knowledge and refused to voice my terror. But, in idle moments, the fortresses of my mind weakened, allowing my thoughts to escape and wander along a terrifying route that presented one horrific scenario after another. Without sight how on earth would I function in a world designed for visual perfection? Seemingly inconsequential things like choosing the right shade of sweater, applying make-up or simply finding my way around the house loomed like gigantic obstacles. Little wonder, with such dire implications, I decided to push the possibility of future blindness to the back of my mind and concentrate on the present where my vision, although impaired, was still intact. Fortunately, there was a lot going on in the world to offer some welcome distraction. Headlines screamed Britain's celebration at the historic election of a female prime minister while America lamented the passing of the much-loved silver screen hero, John Wayne. On the music front, artists like Rod Stewart, Dr Hook and David Bowie were setting the beat for yet another generation of youth.

Despite my original plans, I had to accept that third level education was beyond my visual capability. The long hours of study required for a university degree would place an enormous strain on my already over-taxed sight. In the end I decided that, as I was a qualified life saving teacher and swimming instructor, I should apply for a job as life guard and staff trainer with the Belfast City Council's Leisure Services Department. As a people person, I knew the position would be perfect for me and was absolutely thrilled to learn I had been accepted for the role.

Like most girls my age, I loved to spend weekends at the cinema, shopping or dancing the night away at a local nightclub. Boyfriends were also part of the teenage agenda and although there were no serious relationships, I did have a few transient infatuations! Still, few males, regardless of handsome looks or charming ways, could live up to the latest love of my life. The purchase of my first car, a four-year-old, racy red Mini Estate, was more than a form of transport. To me, she was a passport to independence. Driving was sheer pleasure. The ability to go when and where I wanted without depending on others was wonderfully liberating.

Apart from my beautiful little car, I began to develop a fascination for radio communication. One of my mates, with a shared interest in the scouting organisation, owned a Citizens' Band radio and invited me to join the fun of making friends over the air waves. It was hilarious. We'd spend ages chatting and giggling with other CB enthusiasts, forming a network of good-natured camaraderie. During one of these exchanges, I was introduced to a guy whose name, or, in CB speak, 'handle', was Rover. He seemed so friendly and easy to talk with that when he eventually asked for an 'eyeball', or in other words, a meeting, I just couldn't resist.

As it turned out, Rover's real name was Paul Gray. He was, as I expected, charming, considerate and extremely witty. I think I was smitten from the moment we met, although it did take a while for Cupid to perfect his aim! In the beginning, Paul and I confined our relationship to the platonic variety, preferring to meet as part of a group. However, Paul's initial attempt to move towards a more romantic scenario met with disastrous consequences.

Naturally shy, he decided that, in order to secure a date, he needed an extra dose of bravado. Unfortunately, his choice of morale booster proved a complete turn-off. By the time I arrived at the nightclub, Paul, filled with Dutch courage and rapidly running out of common sense, made the drastic mistake of getting down on one knee and asking me to marry him. Furious at him for making a spectacle on the dance floor, I stormed off in a huff. His friend Billy managed to mollify my annoyance by explaining the poor guy's good intentions. The next day, while Paul nursed his embarrassment as well as a hangover, another guy stepped onto the scene and before long we were a couple. However, I've no doubt that, despite my now having a steady boyfriend, Cupid was determined that Paul Gray and I should end up together. If romance was off the menu, Paul settled for friendship. Quietly and steadily, he set about laying the foundation for what would eventually become my oasis of tranquillity in storms of uncertainty and pain. As soon as I realised my current beau wasn't for me, Paul seized the opportunity to ask me out and eventually the spark of romance flickered into life, moving our relationship to another level. Paul's natural good humour and witty conversation made him great company at any time. But there's no doubt that it was his skill as a water-skier that contributed a thrill of excitement. To me the sport sounded daring, extreme and very cool. Sadly, an accident during training resulted in an injury to his Achilles tendons and unfortunately put paid to any serious participation in the activity.

We'd been dating for almost two years when Paul, this time without the aid of some Dutch courage, finally asked me to marry him. I was ecstatic and had no hesitation accepting his proposal. As our relationship continued to blossom I began to think seriously about our future. I'd already watched Pop and Ian lose their sight and I didn't want to witness a similar fate for our children. If Paul and I had a family, would they too fall victim to the terror of glaucoma? My specialist didn't know the answer and agreed to refer me to a genetic expert, Professor Norman Nevin. I'll never forget sitting in the professor's office listening as he explained the laws of heredity and probability. Despite the doctor's gentle and considerate manner, the truth was a bitter pill to swallow. With 100 per cent odds, it seemed that the next generation in the Snowdon line would face the awful reality of a life in darkness. How on earth could I knowingly give my children such a heritage? Naturally, I explained the prognosis to Paul but he, as always, was optimistic and reassuring, telling me not to worry, everything would be fine.

Making plans for our wedding and saving for a deposit on a house left little money to spend on treats like trips to restaurants or the cinema. Yet Paul and I were content to spend our evenings watching telly or walking his mum's little poodle. In fact, I don't think our tiny four-legged friend had ever pounded the pavement so much in her life. She must have been exhausted! Like any bride-to-be I was looking forward to a new role in life, decorating our home and enjoying the future. Life was good.

The downward spiral began with a seemingly minor accident at work. I was asked to supervise delivery of some new equipment at the centre but in order to get to the store I had to cross the main sports hall, where a football match was already in progress. Waiting for a lull in the activity to make my move, I grabbed the first opportunity to dash between players and cross to the other side. Unfortunately, I failed to spot a guy running toward me, although I certainly felt the impact. Our collision left us both dazed but as his head was a lot harder than mine, I came off worse and for the next few days was off work nursing a severe headache and sporting a couple of shiny black eyes.

It didn't take long to realise I'd suffered more than a few unsightly bruises. After the collision I began to notice subtle changes to my sight. If I stooped to pick something up from the floor, I tended to reach to the side of the object, completely failing to grasp it. At night, my field of vision seemed more restricted than usual so, as a precaution, I avoided driving in the dark. Concerned at the changes, I made an appointment to see the specialist, who agreed that the pressure in my eyes had indeed increased. However, he was quick to reassure me there was nothing to worry about and things would eventually settle. In the past, I had been only too pleased to accept whatever crumbs of medical comfort were on offer. But this time, I couldn't ignore the evidence of my own eyes. I knew my sight was failing at an alarming rate. Desperate for help, I went to see my optician, Mr Edgar, hoping that all I needed was a slight adjustment to my contact lenses and things would return to normal. As soon as Mr Edgar had finished examining my eyes, his expression told me all I needed to know. His advice that I should return immediately to hospital extinguished the last embers of hope.

Pop accompanied me to hospital, trying his best to allay my fears. Mr Cowan, an expert in his field, had been good to the Snowdon family, working frantically to save Pop's and Ian's sight. Ironically, in an era when technology could put

men on the moon, nothing could prevent my family's
blindness. During the consultation, I learned that Mr
Cowan's low key attitude was part of a strategy to ensure my
eye pressure remained as low as possible. According to the
doctor, stress and anxiety are major factors that only
exacerbate the problem. It was in my best interests to keep
me as calm as possible but what medical opinion failed to
take into account was the fact that I had lived with glaucoma.
I knew the symptoms, understood the implications and had
witnessed the devastating results. There was no point in
offering me a prescription for soothing words or spoonfuls
of optimism when what I needed was a huge dose of honesty.
It was time for some straight talking and by the time Pop and
I left Mr Cowan's office, I had had more than my fill.
Apparently, my eye pressure had escalated to dangerous
levels, damaging the optic nerve. The only option was an
immediate operation. Shaking with nerves, I sat in the
hospital canteen, sipping cups of tea, trying to find enough
equilibrium to allow me to drive home. With my heart racing
and waves of nausea threatening to overwhelm me, I tried to
come to terms with the situation. Pop did his best to offer
words that would comfort me. Outwardly he was calm but
inside his heart was breaking as once again another of his
children fell headlong towards the black hole of glaucoma.

Telling Mum that I needed surgery was gut-wrenching.
Although she didn't say anything, one look at her face told
me that inwardly she was screaming. The atmosphere at
home was laden with unspoken anguish as my parents
struggled to maintain a sense of normality. I couldn't bear
their pain and also I needed time to think. After lunch, I
made an excuse to leave the house and, jumping into my
beloved Mini, I headed for a beautiful little spot by the sea,
known as Helen's Bay. Initially as I trekked along the deserted
beach, my head pounded with a jumble of incoherent
thoughts, but gradually the sound of birds calling and the

gentle lapping of the waves worked its magic and I grew calmer. Climbing onto a rock, I sat staring out to sea and allowed the unspoken questions to surface. What would happen if surgery was unsuccessful? How would I cope if I ended up totally blind like Pop and Ian? The prospect was too horrendous to contemplate. Surely God wouldn't let this awful disease strike our family a third time? But what if He did? Images of my mum flooded my mind. She hadn't escaped her portion of sorrow. Watching her husband and young son struggle to cope in a world of darkness had broken her heart. Now, she was faced with yet another blow. Life couldn't possibly be so cruel. Eventually, I returned to the car, my body aching from hours of frozen immobility. What I needed was some level-headed pragmatism and a warm hug. I knew exactly where to find both and headed for Paul's house.

As usual, my fiancé didn't let me down on either count. With his arms around me, he listened as I poured out my fears, then, with characteristic optimism, he managed to turn my thoughts in a more positive direction and even brought a smile to my face. Perhaps things weren't as bad as they seemed and I was worrying needlessly. Over the weekend, Paul made sure we had a hectic schedule that didn't permit any time for thinking about Monday's ordeal.

At last the big day arrived and I was admitted to the familiarity of Ward 28 in Belfast's Royal Victoria Hospital. Mr Cowan came to explain how he intended to operate on my right eye, which was the stronger of the two. He hoped that this procedure would provide the best chance for stabilising the condition and therefore saving my sight. That evening, as visiting hour ended, I walked my parents and Paul to the end of the corridor before kissing them goodnight. After they'd gone, I decided to relax and watch television for a while before going to bed. I had no idea that these small pleasures I'd always taken for granted were about to be snatched away.

Worse still, I would never again see the faces of the people I loved.

The next day, as I regained consciousness, I was still hoping that the operation had been a success. My right eye was bandaged but my left eye seemed equally useless. Squinting and trying to focus, it suddenly dawned on me how bad my sight in the weaker eye had become. Of course, I knew there had been a certain amount of deterioration but with my right eye's ability to compensate, I was unaware of how little sight actually remained. Quickly, I reached for my contact lens and put it into my left eye thinking that it would help bring things a little more into focus. Talk about a shock to the system. When my vision remained unchanged, I think it was the closest I came to a coronary! But worse was to come.

A week later, the bandage was removed from my right eye. At first, I put the total lack of vision down to post-operative trauma. After all, my eye was still painfully inflamed; healing was bound to take time. My consultant's explanation that complications had occurred during surgery added another source of worry. Yet there was nothing I could do but go home and wait for the eight-week recovery period to elapse. I never realised how two short months could seem like an absolute eternity. Of course, they did eventually pass and, as the doctors had promised, the post-operative scars had healed. But, no matter how long I waited, my sight did not return. I hadn't escaped my fate. I, like Pop and Ian, would be blind.

It is impossible to describe my feelings at the realisation I would never see again. As I grieved for my loss, acute fear mingled with intense sorrow constantly engulfed me. Shut in, circumscribed by darkness, I felt trapped and vulnerable. Living with Pop and Ian may have introduced me to the concept of blindness but nothing could have prepared me for the reality. One moment I had been a happy, confident young woman looking forward to becoming a wife. Suddenly everything had changed. The future that had once sparkled with happiness was now shrouded with apprehension and uncertainty. At home all day, I had a lot of time to think and the thought uppermost on my mind was Paul Gray. There was no doubt I loved him and wanted nothing more than to be his wife. But I had to set him free. Glaucoma had ruined my life; there was no way I would allow it to destroy his. Just because we were engaged, I didn't want him to feel obligated or tied to me. Neither did I want his pity.

When I told Paul I wanted to talk to him, he hadn't a clue what was on my mind. We drove to the beach at Helen's Bay and after walking silently along the shore, Paul asked if something was bothering me. Taking a deep breath, I blurted out my decision to call the engagement off. He was utterly shocked. I could hear the pain as well as the confusion in his voice as he repeatedly asked for a reason. What had happened? Did I no longer love him? Was there somebody else? Choking back the sobs, I explained that the only reason I was letting him go was because I loved him and didn't want him burdened with a blind wife. Losing a major sensory organ brings enormous challenges, not only for the person involved but also for their family. As well as emotional and psychological aspects, blindness brings a whole new set of house rules. I'd grown up learning the importance of being tidy, closing doors, etc. I didn't want to place the same daily restrictions on Paul's life. By the time he drove me home, we were both emotionally drained and suffering the pangs of a broken heart.

Over the next few weeks, I refused to answer his calls. Then, one evening, Paul arrived at our home and insisted that I get my coat, go with him and listen to what he had to say. I reckoned that, after calling off our engagement, I at least owed him a sympathetic hearing. After he'd listened once more to all my reasons why we shouldn't marry, he gave me a piece of his mind. It was one of the most eloquent speeches I have ever heard! It went something like this:

> *'Listen here Janet Snowdon, whether you like it or not, I have a say in this too. I love you more than anything else in the world and blindness doesn't alter the fact. With or without sight, you're still the same old Janet and I see no reason why we can't get married.'*

What an impact his words made on me. How on earth could I refuse a man who loved me with such depth and passion? My sight may be gone but there was nothing wrong with either my heart or brain! Paul Gray was a treasure. I loved Paul, if possible more than ever, and even logic dictated I'd be crazy not to marry him. Although, before I could say yes, there was another issue that had to be addressed. We'd broached the subject of children once before but now we needed mutual understanding and clarity. As a carrier of the mutant gene, I had made up my mind to remain childless and spare a future generation the horror of glaucoma. With great tenderness, Paul agreed that our life together would not include children, although, to my amazement, he went on to remove any feelings of guilt or responsibility. Apparently, the Gray family had their own hereditary complications. With a high risk of Prolexia, a condition affecting the brain, Paul had decided he too would forgo the joys of parenthood and spare his offspring from tragedy.

Returning home, I knew the problems associated with losing my sight hadn't gone away. But, even in the darkness, it was impossible to extinguish the little flame of happiness that comes from being in love.

Chapter 3

The Thirty-Nine Steps

Thirty-nine steps may have led the characters in John Buchan's novel to an adventure of espionage and political intrigue but for me, the same carefully numbered strides began at the door of Belfast's Sinclair Seaman's Presbyterian Church and ended at its altar! Situated in the docklands area of the city and used regularly by visiting seamen, the church was our family's regular place of worship as well as the centre of my early social life. Designed by famous architect Charles Lanyon in 1856, the church has a distinct maritime theme. The pulpit, shaped like a ship's prow and flanked by navigational lights, plus an original bell from the World War II battleship HMS *Hood*, add significantly to the seafaring atmosphere. Even the collection boxes bear a strong resemblance to lifeboats. Interestingly, although unknown to me, I had been surrounded by reminders of nature's element that would eventually bring me the gift of freedom.

Apart from swimming and the usual variety of youthful activities, as a young girl I had entertained a few wistful dreams of the day when, dressed in a fairytale wedding dress, I'd walk down the aisle of our church's beautiful and familiar surroundings. I'm not sure whom I imagined as groom but no doubt he was blessed with more than his share of handsome good looks! Regardless of what romantic notions occupied my teenage thoughts, I never envisaged the awful scenario that lay ahead. Never in my wildest imagination did I think my wedding day would be marred by blindness.

Preparations for the wedding began months before the event. As neither of us could see, Pop and I had to come up with a plan that would lead us directly to the altar, avoiding any embarrassing stumbles or collisions along the way. We decided that by counting the exact number of steps and using the pews on either side as guidelines, we should be able to plot a reasonably straight course. Paul and I decided to make it a real family affair by asking those closest to us to play the traditional and major roles. While I invited his sister Ruth to act as bridesmaid, Paul asked my brother Ian to be best man. At just sixteen, it was a lot of responsibility for such a young man but we knew he'd do a great job.

The organisation of any wedding is a hectic period. There just don't seem to be enough hours in the day to get through the endless list of tasks. Yet, with no job and forced to remain home alone, I found time dragged. The problem with solitude is that it leaves the mind free to wander in any direction it chooses. My thoughts constantly headed towards the frightening implications of a life without sight, reducing me to tears and leaving me feeling hopelessly confined to a world of darkness. As well as ending a happy, active career, glaucoma had stolen my independence, and the sale of my beautiful car only added to my misery. I was inconsolable that my little Mini had gone and I would never drive her again. Afraid to dwell on the situation, I tried to make sure I kept as busy as possible and used housework as a means of diversion. Living with Pop and Ian had taught me the importance of routine safety measures but I'd never learned to use a vacuum cleaner or cook a meal without the gift of sight. For some things, the plan was simple enough. Using my memory, I made a mental map of each room, dividing the floor into a kind of carpeted grid before painstakingly moving the cleaner back and forth over each small area until I was satisfied all trace of dust and debris had gone. As my confidence grew, I took up the challenge of ironing a razor-sharp crease in trousers and shirt sleeves until practice, as well as one or two nasty burns, awarded me a fair measure of success. With deftness I would never have believed possible, my hands guided polishing cloths over mirrors and tiles, eliminating even the tiniest smear. I even managed to master the art of hanging curtains. By feeling my way along the top and making sure the tape remained even, I knew the folds of material would fall naturally into place. If they didn't, no-one was ever rude enough to point it out. Cooking was a major challenge. Feeling the heat from a hob or oven is one thing but calculating the actual proximity is a scary prospect that doesn't leave much margin for error. Perhaps more than anything else, blindness instils a fear of fire. The ability to smell smoke and feel the heat from flames yet not be able to pinpoint the source is a nightmare for many blind people. However, glaucoma may have taken my sight, but it hadn't affected my original portion of stubborn determination and before long I had developed a technique to prevent burning the dinner or, more importantly, myself! I quickly learned to put a pot on the ring just prior to ignition, then I'd listen to detect the sounds that distinguished simmering from boiling. Timing was crucial and, with a few trials and errors, I was eventually able to produce some fairly decent meals. Developing household skills provided the distraction I needed and they certainly ensured Paul had a fussy and thoroughly domesticated wife.

As the days ticked by and our wedding day loomed closer, I began to feel a growing sense of apprehension. Adapting to my strange and unwelcome way of life remained an uphill struggle and instead of nuptial anticipation, my moods often lurched somewhere between frustrated annoyance and nostalgic melancholy. I did my best to put on a brave face for my family and Paul but there were times when the full impact of my loss hit with such unexpected force, I was left drowning in fresh waves of panic.

Shopping for my wedding dress should have been a special occasion for me as well as Mum. Every mother wants to see a glow of happiness on her daughter's face as she tries on her special gown. Instead of a radiant bride-to-be, poor Mum was confronted by my mask of disinterested apathy. What she couldn't read was the depth of distress that it just about managed to camouflage when, standing in the salon, dressed in all my bridal finery, I suddenly realised that, regardless of how sensitive or delicate, there are occasions when the sense of touch is no substitute for sight. Mum did her best to encourage me to feel the fabric. But I didn't want to use my hands to capture the image. I wanted to be like other girls and twirl in front of the mirror, admiring the cascades of beautiful white satin as they pooled in shiny folds around my feet. Mum's description of the pretty sweetheart neckline and short puffy sleeves made it easy to imagine, but more than at any other time, I desperately wanted to see. In the end, defeated and upset, I left the choice of dress to Mum. She and Paul also had to select the design for wedding stationery as once again, I didn't want to go through the process of having to feel my way towards choosing a pattern. It must have been an incredibly painful time for those around me as they watched my struggle to accept the restrictions of blindness.

Eventually the big day arrived. On 11 August 1984, our house, like any home on the morning of a wedding, was a flurry of excitement. After Mum and I returned from the hairdressers, she and Ian got ready, scurrying around, making sure everything was in order and nothing had been forgotten. Pop, as father of the bride, waited eagerly to play his important role. A friend, bubbling with enthusiasm and armed with an array of cosmetics, arrived and set about giving me the perfect complexion. Thankfully, I recalled training from part of my Duke of Edinburgh Award course, on how to apply my own make-up, although it did take a while to master the technique of using mascara. Depending on whether or not I aligned the brush properly with my lashes, I either ended up with sore eyes or making a fair impression of a panda. Eventually, I discovered that regular trips to the beauty salon were a great way to save time and hassle. Tinted lashes as well as eyebrows and a perfectly waxed brow line guarantee a neat and tidy appearance, leaving me the minimum of fuss. Although, for more definition, I continued to apply a coat of mascara to the top lashes. I've never worn foundation, so it didn't pose a problem. Lip gloss, on the other hand, is fairly easy to use and in my opinion is a beauty aid no girl can do without. As for blusher, well, apparently all I had to do was smile—with cheekbones duly displayed, it was an easy matter of sweeping upwards and outwards, following the natural contours of my face. The discovery of a Braille Dymo Gun proved an invaluable tool for marking the various lids of individual eye shadow colours.

Thanks to my friend's expertise, my wedding make-up was flawless, although there was nothing anyone could do to disguise my extremely thin figure. At 5ft 8ins, and weighing just 80 lbs, the trauma of losing my sight had certainly taken its toll. With a weakened immune system, I was prone to a series of chest infections that sapped my energy and turned me into a very skinny bride!

As the wedding morning progressed, it seemed the only one immune to the happy ambiance was me. After a night spent tossing and turning, plagued by trepidation and worry, I woke depressed and exhausted. At 11 a.m., I went to my bedroom for the last time and put on my beautiful new dress.

With Gran's lovely necklace, a borrowed head-dress and a pretty blue garter, I had everything needed for the traditional recipe that guarantees a lifetime of wedded bliss. I may have looked every inch an ecstatic bride but I still didn't feel like one. True, my feelings for Paul were as deep as ever and there was no doubt I wanted to spend the rest of my life with him. Yet, I simply couldn't shake the sombre mood. I was frightened and worried about the future. Somehow the thought of change terrified me. Losing my sight had thrown me into a vortex of darkness where I felt disorientated and vulnerable. With hindsight, I was probably trying to hang on to everything that offered comfort and familiarity. Leaving my family home, where blindness was a way of life and everyone understood the rules, was a huge step. Each room, piece of furniture, even the décor was indelibly printed on my mind. It was the one place where I could feel safe. Suddenly, I was stepping into the unknown where I'd not only have to get used to a new environment but share it with a man who, no matter how much I loved him, had no experience of living with a blind person. When everyone had left for the church, Pop, sensing my mood, enfolded me in an enormous hug, told me how proud he was of his little girl and reassured me that everything would be alright. At last the wedding car arrived and, stepping into the August sunshine, I was taken aback by the number of friends and neighbours waiting to pass on their wishes for our future good luck. It was a touching moment and, for the first time that day, my heart began to melt at the display of such warmth and kindness. On the way to the church, Pop and I sat in the back of the limousine, saying little. But in the clasp of my hand he detected my turmoil of emotion and, with a gentle squeeze of my fingers, sent a message of fatherly love and support.

The beautiful sound of bells welcomed our arrival and, at a signal from the minister, the organ roared into life. All the practice paid off and as we sailed up the aisle, silently counting every step, neither Pop nor I put a foot wrong! It was a lovely ceremony and as we'd chosen hymns I already knew well, I was able to join in the singing. Finally, when vows were made and rings exchanged, Paul and I were ushered into the vestry to sign the register for the first time as husband and wife. Although delighted to be Mrs Gray, I couldn't help but feel a slight twinge of sadness. I'd spent two decades of life as Janet Snowdon and now, with a simple flourish of the pen, I was taking on a whole new identity. I remember wondering if other girls felt the same pangs of nostalgia or were mine merely the result of post blindness trauma.

The arrival of my Beaver Scouts, from St Peter's Church of Ireland, to provide a guard of honour outside the church, added a special touch of magic to the day. I'd always loved working with the youngsters and was heartbroken when blindness forced me to resign. Fortunately, Ricky McKnight, our Group Scout leader, came up with an ingenious plan to change my mind. Realising that blindness had severely dented my confidence, he decided to show me that being a good Beaver Scout leader didn't depend on visual ability. I had a great rapport with the kids, knew my way around the hall and was familiar with all the activities involved with scouting. Yet, he was wise enough not to use words as his method of persuasion. Instead, he asked me if I'd mind coming along for a few sessions to show the new leader the ropes. I agreed but, when no-one turned up, I simply carried on as usual. This scenario continued for several weeks until I finally caught on to his cunning scheme. There was no new arrival but by then there was no need to find a replacement; I'd regained my confidence and decided I was the one for the job!

The guard of honour was a lovely gesture and I knew how much the lads must have looked forward to their role. Unfortunately, one little boy came down with a bout of chickenpox and wasn't able to take part. Devastated but determined to add his own congratulations, he persuaded his parents to drive him to the church where he could watch the proceedings from the car. I was so touched by the fact that, despite his disappointment, the youngster made a special effort to think of me. I went over to say a personal thank you and his delight at the unexpected fuss obviously made his day and, for some inexplicable reason, sent a ray of sunshine into mine.

Our original plan to hold the reception at the Belfast Castle had to be changed because of a fire that closed the building for several years. But our decision to celebrate at the Chimney Corner was far from disappointing. The sun shone as we posed for pictures at the wishing well, on a swing or beside an enormous horse and cart. After lunch, the usual speeches were filled with wishes for our future health and happiness. As expected, Ian made a fantastic best man and I had it on Mum's authority that Ruth looked beautiful in her pale blue dress. At the end of the day, I was exhausted. One aspect of blindness that many people overlook is that it is unbelievably tiring. Without sight, the need for continual concentration is sheer hard work. Relaxation or loss of focus, even for a moment, can result in an accident causing serious injury. Little wonder I was happy when, at the end of a long and bittersweet day, we waved goodbye to our guests and allowed a friend to drive us to our new home. Paul and I had decided to postpone our honeymoon and invest all our savings in the purchase of a house. Situated in the Seaview area of North Belfast, where I'd attended school, our first home was in a district I knew well. However, as there was still a lot of renovation to be done, the little house didn't exactly come up to newly-wed standards and so, without telling anyone, we packed our bag, jumped into Paul's car and headed for the scenic routes of the beautiful north coast. Our seaside break may have lasted only a few days but it allowed

Paul and I some much needed time and space to be alone, enjoying our new roles. A few days later, we returned to begin work on our home and look forward to the next chapter in the adventures of Mr and Mrs Paul Gray.

Chapter 4
Married Life

Any departure from the norm, whether it's stretching boundaries, breaking patterns, or simply adapting to a new way of life, is always difficult. No doubt, on her way to becoming the world's first woman to captain a Boeing 747, Beverly Lynn Burns encountered one or two major challenges. Equally, Kathryn D. Sullivan, as the first American lady to walk in space, probably experienced her fair share of nerve-racking moments. I may not have piloted an enormous aircraft or rocketed into orbit but sometimes, as we manoeuvred our way through the pitfalls of married life, it definitely seemed that Paul and I were from different planets!

Getting used to sharing the same living space took time and patience, virtues that were often in short supply. Learning to work together as part of a team is an adjustment that many young couples find difficult but, for us, my lack of vision created an additional strain. Within my family home, where blindness was a way of life, we had all followed a stringent set of rules. From an early age, I'd been taught the importance of ensuring Pop and Ian had a secure environment. I knew that by simply leaving a door ajar or forgetting to put my toys away, I could cause a serious accident. Of course, that's not to say there weren't the occasional moments of carelessness. I'm sure Pop has vivid memories of the time my doll's pram, left at the foot of the stairs, resulted in a fall and a nasty bump on his head. But, by and large, Mum and I adhered to the safety routine and helped avoid unnecessary suffering. When glaucoma eventually claimed my sight, the principles to maximise my safety were already an established part of the Snowdon regime.

However, life in the marital home wasn't so easy. For a start, my physical surroundings seemed strange and unfamiliar. I wasn't used to the layout, especially when we decided that, in order to add a touch of modern comfort, the whole place needed a structural overhaul. The prospect of builders traipsing through the house, especially in the run-up to Christmas, is probably most women's idea of a nightmare but, for me, the army of workmen proved a welcome distraction. My mind's tendency to conjure up images of the past or, more frighteningly, the future, confronted me with painful bouts of nostalgia as well as a dread of the unknown. Occupied with the mundane realities of renovating our house, I had no time to dwell on how life used to be or what it would become. While the builders set about knocking down walls, digging foundations and generally reshaping our home, I scurried back and forward making sure they had an endless supply of tea and biscuits. As the days grew colder, I decided there was nothing like a roaring fire to help raise the temperature. Admittedly, an open fire wasn't a form of heating I knew much about. In fact, it wasn't until we moved into our Seaview home that I discovered its unique warmth and began to love the comforting sound of flames as they crackled and hissed in our tiny hearth. Paul taught me how to set and light the fire, add coal and use the poker to prod it into life. Unfortunately, on one occasion, I was a little too enthusiastic with the amount of fuel and, as I poked among the burning coals, several fell onto the carpet, immediately setting it on fire. Fortunately, the builders heard my screams and came rushing to help. The carpet was ruined but, apart from a slight rise in blood pressure, nobody was hurt. Although our workmen did insist that, no matter how cold, they'd prefer to stick with hot drinks and skip the bonfire!

By the time Christmas arrived, renovations were still far from complete but Paul and I did our best to maintain the seasonal spirit and even purchased our first Christmas tree. Granted, setting it on top of the telly seemed like an act of sacrilege. Such an important and traditional decoration deserved a much grander and more prominent location. Still, with space at a premium, we had no choice but to opt for a more compact version, although the tiny branches did present a few festive problems. Apart from a decent fairy on top, how on earth would Santa fit our presents underneath? The little tree may not have measured up to expectations but we were determined that our first Christmas as husband and wife should be spent at home. Instead of joining either family for lunch we invited a couple of friends to eat at our place. As it turned out, the meal which Paul and I planned and cooked together was a huge success. The company was equally enjoyable, but lack of heating meant that the only Christmas glow came from a gas heater that we trailed from room to room. Fortunately, the practice didn't become a Gray family tradition.

Renovation work, unfamiliar spaces, not to mention my attempt to burn the place down, certainly kept me busy and occupied. Adapting to the new environment was often physically draining but learning to cope with a husband was emotionally exhausting! Despite constant reminders, Paul continually forgot to put his shoes away, left cupboard doors ajar or moved things without telling me. Inevitably, I either ended up with a bang on the head or screaming with frustration at not being able to find something. Unused to living with blindness, Paul found the disciplined routine difficult. Exhausted from a hard day at work, he'd arrive home to help clean up the builders' mess, then we'd both get stuck into making dinner and washing dishes. Tired and stressed, tolerance levels soon plummeted, freezing the atmosphere but bringing tempers to boiling point. It wasn't an easy time for either of us but, gradually, we began to adjust and before long, harmony was restored.

The builders' departure was a cause for celebration. It was time to start shopping, one of my favourite pastimes. Choosing carpet and colour schemes without the aid of sight may seem a daunting prospect. But I know a good bargain when I feel one! Just by running my hand over its gorgeous deep pile, I could tell our new carpet was great quality. Paul supplied the visual description and I was able to imagine our floor covered in beautiful but subtle tones of moss green. Of course, like a lot of men, my husband suffers the occasional bout of colour blindness and doesn't always find it easy to decide on an exact shade. Choosing our sofa seemed to trigger an attack and I'm sure it was contagious because the young salesman seemed just as incapable of telling me whether the upholstery was pale, mint or lime green. Thankfully, I can always call on Mum in such emergencies and, after she assured me it was undoubtedly mint green and would go well with the carpet, I went ahead and bought it. To be fair, Paul's taste in décor was similar to my own and as my confidence grew, I learned to accept and rely on his judgement. However, when it came to shopping for clothes, I was fairly adept at making my own choices. It's not difficult to know when sizes are too big or too small. Memory served to remind me of colours that flatter my pale skin, but steered me away from anything with a large flowery print. Instead of losing interest in fashion, I became fussier than ever and determined that blindness would not affect my appearance. Using a simplistic code, I organised my wardrobe into various groups of trousers, tops, skirts and dresses. Whatever the occasion or regardless of how I was feeling, I always made sure I was smartly dressed and colour co-ordinated. Organising the kitchen cupboards and freezer, although not as enjoyable as sorting my wardrobe, still required some kind of system. Once again, memory played a key role as I learned to arrange tinned goods in neat alphabetical rows. Naturally, there was the odd time when instead of kidney beans I opened a can of peaches, giving chilli con carne a whole new flavour.

Four years later, life had settled into a comfortable routine. The house at Seaview, at one time strange and unfamiliar, now felt like home. Accustomed to each other's idiosyncrasies, Paul and I had developed a close relationship as well as a healthy respect for each other's individuality. With a better understanding of my needs, Paul's consideration and attempts to make life easier for me were fantastic and much appreciated. Apart from the occasional moments when grief for the loss of my sight made an unexpected attack, I felt contented and relaxed. We didn't go out a lot as most of our savings had been poured into renovating the house but when I discovered the 'talking books' facility offered by the Royal National Institute for the Blind, I was immediately hooked. It's a tremendous service and, for the visually impaired, a valuable link to the outside world.

Despite the fact that Paul and I had agreed not to have children, the maternal ache was never far away. My biological clock didn't know I was blind. It didn't account for the difficulties of raising a child without sight; neither did the horror of passing on the mutant gene slow its rhythm. But despite its unstoppable tick, I knew the terror of waiting for darkness and the pain of sliding into its abyss. Even without Paul's contribution to the heredity gamble, the cost of satisfying my maternal instinct was too great a price. Reversing our decision was not an option. Instead I found pleasure in the company of other people's children and adored working with my Beaver Scouts. However, I never expected the joy that the arrival of a tiny, chocolate-eyed beauty would bring or how she would make the Gray family complete!

When Paul suggested that a dog would be good company for me, I was a little hesitant. An allergy to canine hair had already ruled out the possibility of a guide dog but as I recalled the endless walks we inflicted on Paul's mum's little poodle, excitement began to grow. Despite the close contact, I hadn't suffered a single sneeze. I wasn't allergic to the 'toy poodle' breed. Paul immediately put an advertisement in the paper and, as I set off for the Scout hall, I could barely wait for news. At 8 p.m., Paul called to pick me up and told me there had been a few responses to his advert. The first was from a man who lived in the seaside resort of Bangor. We set off immediately and listened to his unusual tale of how, as a builder, he had done some work for a client who, unable to pay, had left him a pedigree pup as reimbursement. It was a strange scenario but from the moment I ran my hands over Toyah's chocolate curls and Paul looked into her velvety eyes, we were smitten. We took her home with us and she immediately became part of the family. I loved to hear her little feet run to greet me or feel the warmth of her body as she cuddled up beside me on the settee. Toyah may not have been the child we once craved but the love and happiness she gave us went a long way towards filling the hole in our hearts.

Just when it seemed life in Seaview couldn't get better, we decided to move. The renovation work had not only added space and comfort, it had also boosted its value. Looking back, our time in the starter home had been a period of adjustment and learning. Newly blind and newly married had presented a lot of challenges for both of us but after four

years we were ready to step out and try something different.
Leaving a familiar area for one I didn't know at all presented
me with the usual problem of finding my way around.
However, unlike the first time when I'd left my parents' home
full of fear and trepidation, I was now emotionally stronger
and eager to be as independent as possible. Moving house
was the catalyst I needed. After discussing the situation, Paul
and I contacted the Department of Health and Social
Services where a team for the visually impaired provided me
with a personal mobility officer. This group of dedicated
people are absolutely wonderful and do a wonderful job. At
first, the thought of using a white cane filled me with dread.
All my life I'd hated to be different and was concerned that
people would stare at me or pass some hurtful remark, but I
needn't have worried. In fact my cane was the best thing to
happen to me as it opened up a whole new world of shopping
freedom. For the first couple of weeks, my mobility officer
took me to a school where, in a controlled environment, I was
introduced to the important concept of 'spatial' awareness.
While I held onto her arm, she walked alongside, describing
the physical layout. Then, using the cane, I walked the route
alone while my helper followed behind. With all senses in
overdrive, I concentrated like mad as I stepped warily up
stairwells, down corridors, round corners, all the time feeling
and listening for changes in floor texture and surrounding
spaces. Large open areas proved most difficult as, without
landmarks such as posts or walls, it was difficult to judge my
position. The mobility expert taught me to align my back
with the wall and then angle my feet towards the direction I
wanted to take. With the mental image of a clock face, I
visualised the various hours, using them as a compass to
guide my steps. Managing to get in and out of a lift was easy
enough as I could hear it arrive and the doors slide open. But,
once inside, going up or down was a bit more complicated,
especially if the buttons weren't clearly defined or there was

no helpful automatic voice. Once I'd mastered the basics, my mobility officer decided it was time to take me outside and teach me to function in a world where I would encounter and have to cope with all kinds of unexpected scenarios. With enormous patience on her part and extreme concentration on mine, we walked around Belfast city centre, memorising and marking landscapes. I learned to use my cane to explore and feel unexpected obstacles as well as negotiating a way round them. After endless repetition and travelling the route backwards as well as forwards, I felt confident I'd be able to find my way to Marks and Spencer or Boots Chemist! Despite the frustration and exhaustion, I managed to complete my course and was pronounced safe to be let loose on the streets of Belfast. What a fantastic feeling to be able to shop on my own again. I often wondered why I hadn't taken the initiative sooner. Although in my heart I knew that I hadn't been ready either physically or emotionally.

My white cane may have given me a certain amount of independence. But it took a borrowed wet suit, a pair of skis and a shout of encouragement from Paul to really change my life. Yet when Paul's Uncle Jimmy invited him for an afternoon's skiing at Long Lough Water-Ski Club in Ballynahinch, the only thing I anticipated was a pleasant weekend. The club, run by his uncle and a few close friends, was where Paul had originally learned to ski but as he hadn't taken part for several years, I knew he'd find the day a lot of fun. I'd always loved being around water and looked forward to sitting in the boat enjoying the sunshine while Paul skied round the beautiful lough. Later that day, when Paul asked if I'd like to have a go, I was stunned. How could I, a blind woman, possibly ski? Still, I was dying to give it a try and once Paul assured me that there was no reason I shouldn't, I couldn't wait to get started.

The next day, I packed my swimming gear and, bubbling with excitement, accompanied Paul to the lough. For the first time since losing my sight, I felt the thrill of anticipation. There was a definite smile on my face and a spring in my step at the prospect of learning to ski. I borrowed a club wet suit and Paul led me down to the jetty where I listened with fascination as he explained that, by putting washing-up liquid into each of the ski bindings, it would make them much easier to slip on. Wow—this was a whole new world to me! With his Uncle Jimmy driving the boat, Paul stood beside me on the dock and explained how I had to keep my arms straight, my knees tucked tight against my chest and toes pointing upwards. As the boat moved slowly away, drawing the ropes taut, Paul, positioned alongside, gave the signal to hit it and I surged forward. The feel of fresh cool air against my face was exhilarating. Concentrating, I kept my arms straight and tried to relax. Then, before I knew what was happening, Paul had grabbed me by the top of my life jacket and shouted, 'Okay, stand up now!' We were off! Suddenly I was skiing around the lough. I couldn't believe it. Somehow, I had pulled it off. On my first attempt I had managed to stand up and ski. Grinning from ear to ear, I kept going, almost afraid to speak to Paul in case I fell and broke the spell. As the boat went into a turn, Paul began to give me instructions but to my amazement I found that the movements came naturally. The subtle changes in the sound of the boat's engine told me when it was about to go into a turn. The skis tracking through water, the wind in my hair and the feel of the rope in my hand seemed to feed my heightened senses. I may not have been able to see but I'd absorbed everything. After three laps, we began to slow and Paul shouted for me to let go. With a natural ease I wouldn't have thought possible, I loosened my grip and sank gracefully into the water. Boy was I on cloud nine! I hadn't been this happy since the day I passed my driving test. Paul's pride in me was the icing on the cake. He was absolutely delighted by my success. Losing my sight had once plunged me into a world of darkness where it often felt cold and alien. Suddenly, the icy chill of loss began to thaw as the warm promise of what I could become told me it was time to live again.

Chapter 5
A New Beginning

In our new home every room came with a view. Situated on the slopes of Belfast's Cavehill, our rear windows overlooked the greenery of a country park while those at the front watched the neon glow of city life. It struck me that just a few years earlier my inability to see either vista would have triggered tears of frustration and fresh bouts of pain. Now, simply by listening to Paul's descriptive narrative, I was able to visualise and find pleasure in our scenic surroundings. There was no doubt I'd come a long way towards accepting I was blind.

Despite the progress, moving house had been a major challenge. Leaving neighbours I knew well for an area full of strangers was a daunting prospect and in the early days at Cavehill, I worried constantly about how people might react to me. I needn't have worried. Thanks to Dorothy, the wonderful lady who lived next door, Paul and I were immediately put at ease and made to feel welcome. By inviting us to supper, our friend tactfully arranged for us to meet other neighbours and completely removed any remaining anxieties. Suddenly, instead of apprehension, the new house provided me with a real sense of achievement, cementing yet another layer of confidence.

Moving from room to room, I enjoyed the sense of discovery and feeling of space. Visualising each layout, I began to play with ideas for re-designing the kitchen and bathroom. As the shapes and patterns formed in my mind, I realised that changing our living environment was no longer a means of distraction, it was fun! I loved stamping the walls and floors with a little touch of individuality, bringing the place to life and turning our house into a home. It was wonderful to take my cane and head for town where, like any other housewife, I spent hours wandering round shops, choosing and fussing over the perfect furnishings. Although, whether it was searching for curtains or socks, shopping could sometimes take a little longer than expected. Very often I went to buy some lacy underwear from Marks and Spencer and came home three hours later with a bottle of aspirin from Boots! It all depended on whether or not 'Joe Public' was in a helpful frame of mind. Unknown to the sighted community, there's an unwritten rule amongst the blind population never to refuse an offer of help. Regardless of how competent or confident the individual, there will always be those for whom lack of vision remains a major problem. Perhaps they are still shocked and shaken by the sudden plunge into darkness, or maybe they haven't yet crossed the bridge towards acceptance. Any display of ungratefulness from those more experienced or adept at negotiating the boundaries of visual impairment could rob others of a valuable source of assistance. In my case, the occasional hijacks by well-meaning individuals were amusing, if a little time-consuming. I've lost count of the number of times I've been marched across roads, escorted down escalators and into shops I'd no intention of visiting. Yet I have to confess that without the highly trained security staff in most of the high street stores, shopping would be a nightmare. As soon as a blind person enters the shop, it's standard practice for the security guard to lead them to a member of staff who is equally willing to act as an escort and provide assistance.

Shopping for our new home proved an unexpected source of pleasure. But in the weeks following the move, my main concern had nothing to do with choosing the décor. All I wanted was to be able to find the place! The Cavehill area may be extremely beautiful but the pavements tend to be long and uphill all the way. Our house was situated on a bend in the road right at the top of a very steep climb. However, like many of the problems I'd envisaged, the solution was a lot easier than imagined. I rapidly discovered that after crossing a road, there were several useful landmarks to guide me home. By stopping to feel railings and hedges, I began to memorise the route. As the gradient increased and the pavement curved towards the left, my hand touched the little privet hedge of the house next to ours, telling me I was almost home. Familiarity with surroundings both indoors and out is the key to safety as well as confidence. Of course, it isn't always possible to anticipate the unexpected, especially if it happens to be a large hole in the pavement. Rushing to keep a hairdressing appointment, I'd no idea there was a deep trench in my path until I fell headlong into it. Fortunately, apart from a few muddy splashes, the only injury incurred was a dented ego. It didn't help when a crew of workmen drew up and shouted a warning to 'watch out for the hole!' The incident eventually became part of a long list of amusing anecdotes, but at the time I couldn't see the funny side.

With a new zest for life, I was happier than I ever thought possible. Paul, elated by the change, encouraged me to develop a sense of purpose and achievement. He'd shared some of my darkest days and knew how far my self-esteem had plummeted, yet, regardless of sombre moods and endless tears, he'd remained constant. Words may have offered little consolation but I was always certain of a shoulder to cry on and a warm hug to help ease the pain. Ironically, the man I had almost torn from my life provided the best environment to allow me to heal. Later, by introducing me to water-skiing, he helped me find a new sense of identity and, for the first time since losing my sight, a feeling of normality.

After the success of my first attempt to ski, I couldn't wait to try again. It seemed ages before the weekend finally arrived and Paul and I could set off for the lough. Toyah, my little toy poodle, liked to come along for the ride, although a brief encounter with a horse's hoof may have dampened her enthusiasm. To be fair, Queenie, our equine friend who lived in a nearby field, wasn't entirely to blame; Toyah did take the first bite. It might have been the sight of Queenie trying to get through the clubhouse door that sparked a bit of canine jealousy. But I think Toyah's decision to nibble the horse's hind leg was prompted by a fit of nervous anxiety. After all, the sound of thundering hooves as Queenie galloped round the field was enough to unnerve anyone. Fortunately, I took the sensible option and stood perfectly still until the horse got fed up and went off for a doze.

Fresh air and a few animal antics made the weekend visit an amusing treat for everyone. But for me, the best part of the day was when, trembling with anticipation, I followed Paul down to the jetty and prepared to repeat the thrill of my last experience on the water. On our second visit, I had an idea that promised to add another dimension of excitement, and when I asked Paul if he thought I could ski alone, his confident assurances were the only encouragement I needed. As soon as the boat's engine reached its powerful pitch, I surged forward and, without help, once again managed to stand up and ski. I'd done it again! Seated in the boat, most of Paul's words were lost in the wind but I knew there was a huge grin on his face. Everything went perfectly. Any notion that my previous success was nothing more than a happy coincidence had well and truly vanished. As I skied confidently round the lough, I knew I'd found my niche.

Losing my sight had brought many unwanted challenges into my life. But having to depend on others was among the worst. Water-skiing went a long way to re-dressing the balance by giving me back a measure of control. On the water there was no difference between me and a sighted skier. The only factor that set us apart was ability and, for the first time, glaucoma couldn't take that away from me. Nothing could dampen my mood; I was euphoric. Apart from personal advantages, skiing provided a sport that Paul and I could share, and before long we were regular participants on the lough and dedicated members of its club.

Saturday at the lough may have been the highlight of the week but I began to notice that other days were also becoming a lot of fun. My association with Social Services led to the formation of Atlanta, a swimming club for the visually impaired. For the first time I was able to meet others who shared my condition. Until then the only blind people I knew were Pop and Ian and, as much as I loved them, our collective or individual loss of sight wasn't an easy topic of conversation. At home, the emotional pain was too raw to risk the damage that words might inflict. Before long, in silent agreement we chose to banish the subject of our blindness into verbal exile. Suddenly, in the company of my new friends, the prohibition was lifted and the taboo removed. What a feeling of relief to be able to not only talk freely, but discover the joy of understanding and empathy. In fellowship born from mutual loss, we could unveil the nightmare of darkness, share its pain or merely enjoy a giggle at some of life's lighter moments. The simple pleasure of talking to another woman whose intimacy with blindness equalled my own was incredibly comforting. To be part of such a group was a privilege and a joy.

As is often the case, the business of life is occasionally interrupted by death. For our family, 1991 brought more than its fair share of sorrow. On 29 August 1991, just four hours apart, both of my beloved grandmothers died. Within ten months we had said a final farewell to eleven members of our family. It was a devastating time. Reeling from the impact, it took a long period of adjustment to come to terms with the grief. Yet regardless of what genes have passed from one generation to another, the dominant one among our family is the survival instinct. In a bid to move on and restore a sense of normality, Mum and I decided to enrol for a few evening classes that offered a course in conversational Spanish. Recording, sifting through, then re-recording the three-hour notes proved a lengthy business but the exercise helped me keep up with my sighted contemporaries and, in the end, Mum and I decided to enter for the more formal qualification of GCSE at ordinary level. We did so well that we went ahead and studied for the advanced version. It was just the distraction and tonic we needed.

My brother Ian had also discovered his sporting passion. As it turned out, my sibling's pursuit echoed my own, although he preferred snow to water. When he persuaded me to go to join a party of blind skiers on a trip to Austria and Germany, I'd no idea it would prove such a fabulous time. We were accompanied by the Royal Dragoon Guards, whose instructors each took a visually impaired member of our group under their wing. It's a huge responsibility as the guide has to watch the route ahead, making sure his or her charge descends the slope in safety. I really loved the experience of ascending the mountain in a chair lift, feeling the icy blast of air on my face. But, on one occasion, coming down the other side wasn't quite as exhilarating. As sod's law would have it, I ended up with the only dyslexic guide in the group. Hurtling along, enjoying the rush, I immediately obeyed the instructor's call to turn left. Before I knew what was happening, my skis had lost contact with the ground and I was flying through the air toward a 25 ft drop below. To say it was a scary moment would be an understatement. I was terrified as I didn't know what was happening or how far I was going to fall. Fortunately, I landed on nothing more sinister than a pile of powdery snow. Despite my shock, I couldn't help but feel a twinge of sympathy for my poor guide who was completely distraught by her error. However, apart from the momentary fright, I loved the whole experience of skiing all day, not to mention the après skiing that occupied most of our nights.

Back home, my diary had never been so full. As well as my involvement with the swimming club, I had agreed to help raise the profile of visual impairment by giving a few talks at local churches and schools. It felt great to be doing something that would benefit both the blind community and the public at large. Without information or knowledge about the problems associated with lack of vision, it is difficult for sighted people to understand or help. I was only too happy to offer some much needed enlightenment. Weekends were still reserved for skiing and I dreaded the end of the season when the opportunity to get out on the water would be temporarily suspended. Sadly our days at Long Lough Water-Ski Club were numbered after a jet-ski operation offered a lot more money than we could afford for access to the lough. Eventually, and with great sadness, we were forced to close. For me skiing had become more than just a sport. It was the only area of my life where I felt totally free and independent and there was no way I was going to give it up. Paul was equally determined to carry on enjoying our shared interest and, after a lot of discussion, we decided to buy a boat. Our choice of a red 16 ft Fletcher with a 75 hp outboard engine caused a lot of excitement and, whether on the waters of Lough Neagh or the River Bann, Paul and I took enormous pleasure from our new toy. Our next purchase was a Bayliner, or as we affectionately called her, 'Binliner'. At 22 ft long with a 90 hp outboard engine, this was a much more powerful craft that allowed us to combine sport with entertaining and socialising. Very often we'd invite family and friends to sample the scenic delights and lovely fresh air of Lough Neagh. While they enjoyed the cruise, I managed to fit in some skiing by jumping off the back of the boat and doing a few laps round the lough. It was a brilliant time for all of us.

But gradually I began to notice that Paul was missing out on some of the fun. As the only sighted person capable of driving the boat, he was unable to ski. It didn't seem fair so we talked it over and came up with a solution.

In 1994, news of the Channel Tunnel which joined England and France occupied the headlines. In Northern Ireland, the IRA had announced a ceasefire and Celine Dion was singing about the power of love. Everywhere, the future beckoned with a promise of hope and prosperity. In keeping with the air of progress and happiness, our decision to join the Meteor Waterski Club, the biggest in the Province, was to prove more than a means to enable Paul and I to share a hobby. It was to change the direction of my life and launch me on a career I never would have believed possible.

As the only blind skier at the club, I found the first season particularly difficult. While most of the members were polite and friendly, there were some who felt awkward and didn't quite know how to approach me. Socially, I didn't mind, as I could always take the initiative and instigate conversation. However, on the water it was a different matter. Somehow, my inability to see was interpreted as physical fragility and the drivers on board were often reluctant to give the throttle I needed, with the result that I didn't always have sufficient power to get going. It was incredibly frustrating. In the end, my pleas to 'just hit it' paid off and gradually they began to understand that blindness doesn't mean weakness.

During my time at Meteor I learned to ski to the command of a whistle. Previously, I'd relied on basic signals to Paul to let him know when I was tired or merely wanted to stop, but at Meteor the whistle was the chosen means of communication between skiers and boat crew as it was the only sound that could be heard above the drone of the engines. The simple series of short blasts or a long continuous shrill told us everything from when it was time to ski, move into a turn or simply let go and sink into the water. It was a system that worked amazingly well.

Joining Meteor was the best thing to happen to both of us. Paul was able to enjoy his sport again while I learned to perfect my technique. Within a short space of time, I'd finally convinced the drivers of the boat that I wouldn't physically break if they stepped up the power. In the early days, I'd learned to get up on two skis and then cut left and right either side of the wake. Yet on joining the club, I discovered that blind skiers do what is known as 'wake slalom'. The exercise is a fast, tight, narrow rhythm where the skier must cross each wake as many times as possible within twenty-five seconds. There are two twenty-five-second passes in tournament and, on two skis, individuals can score two points on crossing, whereas on one ski it's three points on crossing.

My inability to see the wake meant I had to rely completely on the feel of its apex as well as the downward glide. Undoubtedly, it was a difficult process but as my confidence grew so too did my skill. I have to confess that sometimes, the harder I tried, the more difficult it seemed and frustration often set in. However, at the end of the day, perseverance won out. Regardless of complications or how complex the technique, I simply loved to ski.

Our club secretary, Paul McCandless, introduced me to the 'trick' skis. Despite his assurance that it was a relatively easy technique that simply required me to feel for the 'bubbly' bits, I was completely out of my depth. The 'trick' skis were a huge challenge but I refused to let them get the better of me. I knew it was only a matter of time before I got the hang of things. Learning to master this particular discipline was far from easy but no doubt my initial attempts provided onlookers with a lot of entertainment. Eventually, I did manage to get the better of the unfamiliar skis and, to my delight, was soon jumping back and forth over the wakes. It was a fantastic feeling.

Northern Ireland's inter-club event called 'the Northern League' was to be my first taste of success. Intended as an introduction to tournament for novice skiers, the competition was a friendly and relaxed affair. Paul was skiing for Meteor and, initially, my only role was to make tea and coffee for participants and club members. However, when Mid Ulster discovered they had a man down, it was decided I should fill the gap. I could barely believe my ears when the club secretary rushed in and asked me to get my ski kit and head for the jetty. As I pulled on my wet suit, I'm not sure what was uppermost in my mind but I'm certain there were one or two concerns regarding my sanity. Paul's reasoning that it was just a competition for novices, and more about having fun than any display of skill, mollified and reassured me. I eagerly joined the Mid Ulster team and prepared to show Meteor what we could do. To my delight and amazement, we actually won! My home club may have jokingly branded me a 'traitor' but they nevertheless presented us with a lovely little trophy that continues to evoke fond memories. While merely a light-hearted and amusing event, the Northern League inter-club competition proved a turning point in my career. From that moment I developed a taste for winning. I was hooked. On reflection, I can trace the origins of my competitiveness to that day when, instead of making tea, I sliced my way through the waters of Lough Henney at Boardmills and found a purpose and direction for my life.

Chapter 6
Competition Fever

Fifteen years after losing my sight, life finally tipped the balance of happiness in my favour. My involvement with both the Atlanta Swimming Club and the committee of the Northern Ireland Blind Sports had introduced me to other realms of excitement and fulfilment that, just a decade ago, I wouldn't have believed possible. As well as meeting other visually challenged individuals, I was able to experience the various sports our association had on offer. Riding tandem cycles was one of my favourites but ten pin bowling definitely wasn't for me. To be honest, I never quite got the hang of the throwing technique and, no matter how much I tried, would never have won any medals for the effort. My brother Ian, as the committee's representative for snow skiing, instigated an annual trip to the continental slopes which was always breathtaking and usually hilarious. On one occasion, my chum agreed to take a few photos of our ski party using my camera. Imagine my horror when, on returning home, I passed around the images of what I thought was some spectacular scenery only to discover the one causing most interest was a line-up of our members' bare buttocks. I guess that as a 'moon' it could technically be called a scenic shot!

Undoubtedly, one of my greatest discoveries during this period was friendship. As my husband and soul mate, Paul was, and still is, top of the list. Yet I revelled in the discovery of female company. Over the years, I've met many women who have been a wonderful source of inspiration and encouragement but in those early days, it was my good friend Mina from the Atlanta Club who was a real tonic. No matter what was on our agenda, we could be sure to find laughter somewhere on the schedule. Despite being registered as blind, Mina could see in monochrome and had never witnessed the vast spectrum of our Technicolor world. The ability to see, albeit in black and white, meant Mina didn't need a guide dog or a cane to get around but, as we rapidly discovered, she did require assistance when choosing a pair of gloves to match her ski suit. I've no idea what the shop assistant made of the woman who was obviously blind yet insisted on advising her apparently 'sighted' friend concerning colour co-ordination. While Mina and I discussed the merits of blue gloves with a jade suit, the note of incredulity in the young woman's voice confirmed what we both suspected. She was utterly baffled! It can be difficult for the general public to appreciate there are many kinds of visual impairment. Most assume that total blindness is the only outcome when in fact there is an enormous fluctuation in the kind of restrictions various conditions impose on sight. By the time we'd made our purchase and left the shop, the sales assistant remained thoroughly confused and we couldn't speak for laughing.

As well as providing an opportunity to socialise, the Atlanta Swimming Club had a more serious goal. We tried to help others, especially those with a recent diagnosis of sight impairment, to come to terms with their condition. The loss of such a major sensory organ damages more than the individual's ability to see. Apart from a driving licence, it takes away independence, shatters careers and can even destroy relationships. At the Atlanta group each of us understood that there is no short cut to recovery. It is a journey that leads through pathways of grief and everyone must travel at their own pace. By offering advice on how to find re-training schemes, education or some financial assistance, we could equip people with the tools to build a new life. However, in the early days of loss, it is usually emotional support that is most in demand. Very often, a couple of us would arrange to meet the person concerned for a coffee and a chat. The informal setting and sympathetic ear acted as a kind of safety net that helped release the dam of pent-up frustration and fears. It was great to leave our new friend in, if not a happier frame of mind, at least a more positive one. At the end of the day, talking to someone who is able to empathise is the best form of therapy. I know it certainly would have helped me.

Working with my friends at Atlanta as well as those at Northern Ireland Blind Sports gave my life a sense of purpose. Meeting new people was a constant source of pleasure but most of all I loved the feeling of unconditional acceptance. For over a decade, blindness had imposed restrictions and curtailed my freedom yet one of the biggest burdens was the isolation that came from being viewed as different. As a school girl, I'd struggled so hard to maintain a semblance of normality and tried desperately to fit in with my contemporaries. Yet, despite my efforts, glaucoma eventually won. My friends, unsure how to handle the new situation, felt awkward and embarrassed around me. Perhaps frightened at upsetting me or triggering an emotional outburst, they tended to avoid the subject of my blindness. In the end, it was much easier to avoid me.

Suddenly, instead of being an oddity, I was part of a community that regarded blindness for what it is: an unfortunate and tragic fact of life. Of course, it can be scary and nobody attempted to undermine the difficulties; neither did they shy away from discussing the problems loss of vision creates. It felt so good to be able to talk about the things I normally kept locked in my heart. One of the most amazing discoveries was the fact that visual impairment doesn't mean exemption from fun or happiness. Naturally, the more serious aspects of sight loss were a frequent topic of discussion but we didn't neglect to share the funny anecdotes of life's lighter moments. One story that was always sure to raise a laugh concerned my brief encounter with the law when I used my cane to explore a policeman's legs. To be fair, I'd no idea what was blocking my entrance to Marks and Spencer but, with characteristic determination, I set about finding out. Initially, I assumed it was an advertising panel and, as I'd been taught, I used my cane to give every inch a thorough examination. Satisfied there was no danger, I moved around the object and entered the shop where, to my amazement, I was greeted with peals of laughter. My friend solved the mystery by explaining that shoppers had been stopped in their tracks, open-mouthed with amazement as they watched me carry out an impromptu search on an officer of the law. In the circumstances, my mistake was understandable, but I can only guess as to why the red-faced constable didn't put a halt to the proceedings!

My work on the committee certainly offered routine and structure. Nevertheless, it was water-skiing that provided the magic ingredient and added a touch of zest and passion to my life. After the success of the Northern League competition at Meteor, I couldn't wait for the season to begin. Being part of the club's skiing fraternity was a huge boost to my ego and when it was suggested I compete in the Irish Nationals competition, it was a challenge I couldn't resist—although I hadn't reckoned what the decision would do to my nerves. Paul as usual was over the moon with the idea and gave me all the support needed. Ever solicitous of my welfare, my husband always managed to tread the fine line of constant encouragement with ultimate safety. He'd taught me the importance of listening for signals and I'd grown used to the shrill note of a whistle, which is one of the few tones that can be heard above the noise of a boat's engine. The formula was simple but clear. One sharp blast told me it was safe to begin skiing, two consecutive ones indicated the boat was about to go into a turn and I needed to move in behind it. A long, continuous note heralded the end of the session and told me it was time to go home. As a blind skier, I relied entirely on protocol and had the greatest respect for those driving the boat, especially when it was Paul at the wheel. I trusted him implicitly. His years of experience had earned him a reputation as one of the best water-ski instructors around. But just as husbands aren't always the best people to give their wives driving lessons, Paul and I occasionally found the teacher/pupil relationship a little bumpy, especially during wake slalom practice. His demands for perfection combined with my impatience often ignited a few less than romantic sparks. Thankfully, the slalom course was at the other side of the lake and well out of public earshot.

The day for my introduction to tournament competition at National level eventually arrived to find me a bundle of nerves and wondering if insanity had ever troubled my ancestors. Questions like why had I agreed to such a stomach-churning experience and could somebody possibly get me out of here, ricocheted around my head. The event was held at Baron's Court Water-Ski Club just outside the bustling town of Omagh. With an Irish weather front that hovers somewhere between drizzle and torrential downpour, I'd been expecting rain but, apart from a few grey clouds, the expected deluge didn't arrive. Although I'm fairly certain that climatic conditions had no bearing on the sudden bout of shivering that occurred every time I thought of competing in front of strangers. Until now, I'd only ever skied in front of familiar faces at our Meteor Club and while it was great to meet new competitors, I couldn't help but feel self-conscious and awkward. Huddled in front of the clubhouse fireplace, I felt sick with apprehension. Paul could sense my anxiety but did his best to calm and reassure me. In fact, the only one apparently unaffected by the crackle of nervous tension was Toyah. My little toy poodle went to all the events and was well used to accompanying Paul in the boat. She even had her own wardrobe of doggie life-jackets. At Baron's Court, she was wearing a lovely shade of red and seemed pleased by the admiring glances as well as the fuss. While Toyah enjoyed the attention, I continued to shiver and shake, unable to get heat into my body. Still, there was no escape. Whatever the outcome, I had to go through with it. After all, I hadn't travelled almost eighty miles to toast my toes in County Tyrone. Ignoring my heaving tummy, I put on a brave face and made my way to the dock, determined to give it my best shot.

Slipping my feet into the ski bindings, I forced myself to forget the nerves and concentrate on the job in hand. Competing in the discipline wake slalom, I'd practised enough times to know exactly what was expected. Skiing from left to right, then turning hard, I'd have to cross each boat wake as quickly and as many times as possible. However anxious beforehand, out on the water there were no distractions and once again I was in my element. With the wind and spray on my face, I remembered everything I'd learned and put it into practice. Before I realised what was happening I heard the whistle blow to signal the end of the session, and, to my amazement, I'd completed both passes and qualified for the finals the following day. I think I must have ditched the nerves in the first round because I skied much better in the last phase and went on to win my category v1, the classification used for skiers who are totally blind. I was thrilled and Paul was so proud of me. She didn't say

anything but I got the impression Toyah was equally
delighted with my performance. My parents, neither of
whom are the least bit sporty and who had never considered
my skiing as anything other than a hobby, began to grasp the
skill involved and were absolutely delighted for me. Receiving
my prize, a beautiful Tyrone Crystal goblet, was an incredible
moment and very emotional. Even today it holds pride of
place in my trophy cabinet. That evening Paul and I joined
the other competitors in a celebratory dinner. It was such a
fantastic feeling to be part of the wider skiing fraternity.

Winning the National Championships did wonders for my
confidence, not to mention my ego. It also qualified me for
the international level of water-ski competition. The
following season, I would fly to Denmark to be among the
competitors in the European, African and Middle East
Championships. What began as a weekend hobby was about
to become a full-time career. I didn't know it at the time but
my success at Baron's Court Water-Ski Club had launched
me on a course that would eventually lead to some of my
greatest achievements. It would also take me to depths of
despair I could never have imagined. Thankfully, as we
giggled and joked, basking in the afterglow of success and
cosy camaraderie, the future remained shrouded in mystery.

Back home in Belfast, the buzz gradually faded and it was
time for some serious work. With the international
competitions in sight, I knew I'd have to get as much practice
as possible if I wanted to be in with a good chance. When the
Ulster Sports Trust (now the Mary Peters Trust) offered me a
grant of £300 for a week of intensive training in the south of
Ireland, I jumped at the opportunity. I have to admit that the
prospect filled me with excitement but the flight from Belfast
to Cork added a few unexpected thrills. With my slalom ski
stacked behind the pilot's seat there wasn't much room for
manoeuvre. Tossed about on pockets of air, the little six-
seater aircraft felt more like a rollercoaster ride than any form

of aviation transport. I was glad when we finally touched down and I was able to straighten up and stretch my legs. Still, by the end of the week the experience of intense and professional training had proved well worth the effort. Before coming to Cork, I'd recently learned to 'mono slalom ski' but within a few days of my arrival, the improvement in my technique was dramatic. I had a great time in Cork and appreciated all the hard work that went into preparing me to ski competitively as well as helping to develop my skill.

Nineteen-ninety-six could be described as the year I came down with a severe bout of competition fever and never really recovered. Training was long and tiring with hours of practice in water that was often extremely chilly. Yet I loved the sense of achievement when, after pushing myself to the limit, I was rewarded with success. In the outside world, life continued to throw the usual portion of political wrangling into the media melting pot. A freak ice storm and the summer Olympics added a touch of American spice. But regardless of what went on locally or abroad, the year held only one topic of global intrigue. Almost two decades earlier, the world had watched the romantic wedding of a prince and his beautiful princess. Sadly, the fairytale ended in divorce and once again Diana and her ill-fated marriage dominated the news. At one time, it hadn't mattered what went on around me. Whether it was royal celebrations or even those from within my family circle, nothing could penetrate the darkness of my personal loss. Losing my sight had locked me in misery. Fifteen years later I was well and truly free and nothing could dampen my appreciation or enthusiasm for life as I prepared to step up a level in the ladder of water-skiing success.

Chapter 7
Aiming High

The days leading up to the European, African and Middle East Water-Ski Championships were filled with long hours of practice and endless cups of coffee. Water sports are tremendous fun and great exercise but they can be a little on the chilly side. As soon as I'd finished for the day, the first thing I wanted was some internal warmth and I rapidly discovered that, when it came to providing an inner glow, it was hard to beat a cup of hot espresso. However, a daily infusion of caffeine, especially when it's fourteen times a day, can have a few unwanted side-effects. My coach eventually decided to ban the caffeine and abruptly cut off my supply. While I rarely question professional advice, I really missed my cuppa during practice sessions and on one occasion decided to smuggle a travel kettle and a tiny jar of the forbidden granules into my hotel room. At the first opportunity, I slipped back to the room and put the kettle on but just as I was enjoying the illicit brew, my coach arrived sooner than expected and interrupted the pleasure. Before opening the door, I dashed to the bathroom, threw the coffee down the sink, swilled some mouthwash and sprayed the air with perfume. If Coach hadn't plonked his rear end on the hot kettle stand, he never would have guessed my guilty secret or read me the riot act!

Eventually I would become the first disabled athlete on the lottery funding programme but in the early days, it was Paul and I who shouldered the full financial outlay. In a bid to avoid unnecessary expense we tried to arrange our holidays around competition dates and venues. In 1997, as we packed our bags and headed for the airport, I couldn't help but wonder if our trip to Denmark would produce more than a few happy memories. As Ireland's representative in the European, African and Middle East Disabled Water-Ski Championships, I really wanted to do well. However, at one point, it seemed that the chance to compete in the championships as well as our Scandinavian holiday were about to become casualties of an airline strike that threatened to keep us grounded in Northern Ireland. Fortunately, the dispute was resolved and Paul and I heaved a huge sigh of relief when we arrived, safe but totally exhausted, on Danish soil.

Competition day dawned and, as usual, I was a bundle of nerves. Despite excitement at the prospect of competing in an international tournament, I couldn't shake the familiar feelings of apprehension and dread. Apart from an introduction to a new level, the event was also the first time I had competed in two disciplines, wake slalom and tricks. When my name was called as the next skier on the water, I thought I was literally going to be sick. What had originally seemed a good idea once again appeared like complete madness. But, like before, as soon as I was out on the water, I forgot everything except the job in hand. I was determined to pull out all the stops and represent Ireland to the best of my ability. When the final whistle blew, I knew I'd given a pretty good performance but it wasn't until I was presented with a silver medal for the slalom and a bronze for tricks that I realised I'd done better than anyone expected. It was an incredible experience and I was thrilled. Paul was so proud and found it impossible to hide his delight. As the jump event was being held the following day, I knew I wouldn't have to ski and could afford to relax and enjoy some serious celebrating with Paul and a couple of friends. In the village we wandered around looking for somewhere to get the party under way but everywhere was closed. Still, we refused to abandon the search and in the end stumbled across the only pub in the area with opening hours that extended beyond 9 p.m. Interestingly it was an Irish bar and proved the perfect setting for such a perfect occasion. The next morning, as Paul and I prepared to leave the hotel and spend the day at a gentle pace suited to our fragile condition, one of the officials approached me and asked if I'd mind fetching my slalom ski, as a demonstration event had been arranged for a party of blind skiers. I couldn't refuse to participate in the performance but oh my poor head!

We returned to Belfast in a euphoric state of mind. Our family was ecstatic at the news of my achievement and the phone rang constantly as friends called to offer congratulations. A week after our return, I answered the phone, expecting it to be yet another well-wisher. To my amazement, it was the chief representative of the tournament selection committee who told me I'd qualified for the World Championships. He went on to ask if I could be in Florida within ten days. Incredibly there wasn't a tremor in my voice as I readily agreed. It was only after I'd replaced the phone and repeated the conversation to Paul that panic set in. After the recent trip to Denmark, there was no way we could afford a visit to America. But as soon as our wonderful friends and family heard about the dilemma, they rallied round and helped with the finances.

Paul's hectic work schedule made it impossible for him to accompany me to Florida and in the end we decided there was only one option: I would have to go alone. It was a daunting prospect and to be honest, I wasn't the only one who entertained some uneasy qualms. My parents worried constantly, not only about me travelling such a long distance without Paul but how I would manage to find my way around in a strange country. Ironically, at one time, even the thought of moving to an unfamiliar house was enough to throw me into emotional turmoil. Now, with only my friendly cane for guidance, I was contemplating boarding a plane bound for America. Nevertheless, it's amazing how far determination can take a person. Having a dream is also a pretty good incentive and, with a combination of both, the possibilities are endless.

The World Disabled Water-Ski Championships were held at Sunset Lakes, which is the Jack Travers Ski School, a lovely place situated just outside Orlando. As it turned out, travelling alone didn't pose a problem but, as the only flight available was a day ahead of schedule, my arrival in Florida before other team members was fairly intimidating. It was also very hot and humid and I couldn't wait to get to the air-conditioned comfort of my hotel room. But simply finding my way to reception turned into a mini-marathon that left me walking aimlessly around the building. Despite asking clearly for directions, no-one seemed able to understand me. The mystery was eventually solved when a member of staff, realising the difficulty, explained that the problem was due to a simple difference in transatlantic language terms. Enquiries concerning 'reception' may have been greeted with total incomprehension but as soon as I mentioned 'the front desk' I was told exactly where to go.

The arrival of other competitors and team members added to the atmosphere of excitement and anticipation. Once again, it was great to meet those who shared my passion, while stories of the difficulties many had overcome never failed to inspire me. They were a fantastic bunch of people. Of course, as in all walks of life, there are always those who tend to upset the natural balance of harmony. Like the proverbial thorn in the flesh, they can be a constant source of irritation, and, much to my annoyance I found one in our American hotel. The battle for control of the air-conditioning switch began in earnest when I lost my cool with a competitor who, in temperatures of over forty degrees Celsius, insisted on having additional heat in the room. The thought of searing hot nights, not to mention the insect life they attract, was more than I could bear but needless to say, my streak of stubborn determination ensured I won the argument and both atmosphere and tempers finally returned to cooler and more comfortable levels! That evening, when I rang Paul, I told him about the incident and we both had a chuckle. The idea of a tug of war competition in the middle of a ski camp seemed hilarious.

I'd never visited Florida prior to losing my sight and had no memory to help visualise the scenery but I was fairly certain the sky was denim blue, sunshine sparkled on water and an abundance of subtropical flora and fauna dotted the landscape. What I did not envisage was a local resident by the name of George. From the moment I arrived, the guys warned me to stay away from him as he ate girls like me for dinner. I was curious as to the identity of the skier who appeared to have such a bad reputation and wondered which country he represented. The discovery that, far from being an American Romeo, George was actually an enormous alligator that liked to swim in the lake was a bit of a shock. Still, I owe a lot to George. The thought of his hungry jaws snapping at my heels was a great incentive to make sure I stayed on my skis and remained upright in the water. Little wonder I came home with a bronze medal for my performance in wake slalom.

The experience in Florida was incredible. Apart from achieving a new level of success, I discovered I could cope quite well on my own in strange and unfamiliar surroundings. What a boost for my sense of independence. I'd also met a lot of international skiers and made some wonderful and long-lasting friendships. Nevertheless, I really missed Paul and, at times, felt extremely lonely without him. We'd always shared in the fun and excitement of competing and, although we spoke every night on the phone, it often seemed empty without him. I was used to spending the time between skiing sessions, talking over the highlights, enjoying dinner and simply having a laugh. Telephone conversations, while appreciated, weren't as much fun. Instead of with my husband, my free time was spent by the hotel pool with only a Terry Pratchett novel for company. It was great when I finally arrived home and we got together and enjoyed a real family reunion.

December 1997 arrived with the usual spree of Christmas shopping, although I'd more than turkey and tinsel on my list. My nomination for the Belfast Telegraph Sports Award by our Meteor Club provided an excellent reason to buy a new dress. I may not have expected to win anything for sporting ability, but I could get a mention in the fashion stakes! Mum and I toured the high street searching for something special. We were exhausted but finally settled on a deep red, tight-fitting design with a sexy split up one leg. Silver and diamanté accessories completed the outfit and when Paul gave an appreciative whistle, I knew he approved.

I simply couldn't wait for the evening to arrive and when we finally walked into the lobby of Belfast's Europa Hotel, I was beside myself with excitement. The building, despite its reputation as the world's most bombed hotel, had not only survived intact but maintained its original air of dignified grandeur. I guess that, like many of its guests that evening, the famous hotel is one of life's survivors.

Taking our seats, Paul squeezed my hand and gave me a running commentary on the various celebrities and what they were wearing. I may not have been able to see the glitz and glamour but I missed none of the detail. I'd never been to such a prestigious event with so many famous people in one room. In fact, I was so overwhelmed that I didn't even notice Paul's momentary disappearance. When the nominations for the category of Sports Personality of the Year with a Disability were read, I listened intently, wondering which of my contemporaries would win. Never in a million years did I expect it to be me. Unaware that the BBC had trained their camera on my face and managed to capture the expression of shocked disbelief, I got unsteadily to my feet and allowed Paul to lead me to the platform, where Jackie Fullerton and Suzanne Dando presented me with a gorgeous bronze trophy. That evening, the champagne flowed as we continued to celebrate into the wee small hours. Normally Paul and I tell each other everything but that night he was forced to confess that during his brief absence from our table, he'd been told the results and sworn to secrecy. It was his job to make sure I got safely to the platform to receive my prize. Naturally, I forgave him, although it wouldn't be long before I had a little secret of my own.

The New Year began with a week's skiing on the Austrian pistes. It was an energetic start to 1998 but, as the months progressed, the pace showed no sign of slowing. My association with Northern Ireland Blind Sports had introduced me to a number of sporting activities and it wasn't long before I'd added a few more interests to my list. Among my favourites was learning to sail with the organisation known as Visually Impaired Sailors. A natural water baby, I took to life on the waves with ease and had no trouble finding my sea legs. Paul, on the other hand, found the heaving movement of a small craft had a similar effect on his stomach and decided a sailor's life wasn't for him. While my other half remained on dry land, I grabbed every opportunity to join my friends on deck and sail across the Irish Sea as far away as Scotland or the Isle of Man. On one occasion, we boarded the *Lord Rank*, a 68 ft Oyster Rigged Ocean Youth Club Vessel at

Carrickfergus Marina and sailed to the Inner Hebrides. The week-long voyage was hard work but extremely good fun. The *Lord Rank* was certainly a fantastic experience but the highlight of my sailing career was an opportunity to work as part of the crew aboard the Jubilee Sailing Trust ship, the *Lord Nelson*, and spend a week exploring the waters around the Canary Islands. Accompanied by my good friend Susan Curry, who is also blind, and our mutual guide and friend Edwin Dunlop, we flew to La Palma and joined the ship at Puerto Rico.

The *Lord Nelson* is a 188 ft training ship with four masts and no winches. It may not mean a lot to the lay person, but basically the vessel relies on old-fashioned manual techniques and is incredibly hard work. The crew was comprised of twenty able-bodied members who were each teamed with a disabled partner to work four hourly shifts with the same number, in a twenty-four hour period, allocated to rest and relaxation. Only the captain's call for 'all hands on deck' was enough to interrupt our beauty sleep. I shared a cabin with my buddy Sabina and was immensely relieved when she took the bottom bunk and allowed me the less claustrophobic upper one.

At first, sailing may seem an unsuitable pastime for those coping with a physical challenge. However, the *Lord Nelson* is specially designed to make the experience available to everyone in the community, regardless of disability. With a strapping that runs along the centre of the deck, individuals with visual impairment needn't worry about colliding with scuttles or falling over ropes. There are even stairlifts to cater for wheelchair users, while hoists enable those with a physical problem to experience the thrill of going up the main mast to the crow's nest. Climbing high into the rigging was awesome. Lack of vision may have prevented me from seeing how far I'd climbed above sea level but as voices grew fainter, I knew exactly where I was and enjoyed every moment. I was never afraid. The sea held no terror for me. When the going got particularly rough, wheelchairs could be locked into safety points on the deck, ensuring no-one slipped overboard.

As well as the joy of being on water, I loved the feeling of team membership where everyone has to pull together. However, my favourite place on board ship was always at the helm. Visually impaired sailors use an audio compass to plot and steer course, but, whether sighted or not, taking the helm in force 12 hurricanes is a scary experience. Call me weird, but for me it was the thrill of my life! Initially, there was no sign of the approaching storm. As far as I was concerned it was a beautiful day. The sea was calm with not even a breeze to ruffle my hair, but the captain didn't share my opinion and explained that we were what in nautical terms is known as 'becalmed'. I'd no idea what he meant but it didn't take long to find out. Before I realised what was happening the wind had started to howl and, according to my friends, had whipped the waves into a frightening mountain of water. It was too dangerous for wheelchair users to be on deck, but for me, standing at the helm feeling the movement of the boat as it rode the elements was the experience of a lifetime and I was so grateful to the captain for allowing me the privilege. It took over four hours to round the northern coast of Tenerife. Once on shore, Susan and I scoured the local markets searching for bargains. I even had the chance to put my language skills into practice and, after some intense haggling, was rewarded with a lovely leather belt for less than half the original price.

Edwin had taken a lot of slides depicting the voyage and on our return, we toured the Province's yachting clubs giving talks to help raise funds for the Jubilee Sailing Trust and its latest sailing ship, the *Tenacious*. It was so good to give back a little for the fabulous experience we'd enjoyed so much.

Chapter 8
Eastern Delight

The practice of holding ski competitions at different locations meant that Paul and I travelled a lot and were able to visit some amazing places. But neither of us had ever been to the exotic Middle East. Neither had we enjoyed the pleasure of hob-nobbing with royalty! When it was decided that the 1998 European, African and Middle East Championships were to be hosted by King Hussein of Jordan, we couldn't wait for our adventure to begin. The king, with a reputation as an accomplished aviator, motorcyclist and tennis enthusiast, was also a fan of water sports, including skiing, and took a great personal interest in the competitions.

From the moment we arrived in London and found a special flight waiting to fly the European skiers to Amman, the capital city of Jordan, we knew this was an experience we'd never forget. Naturally, the competition was foremost in our minds but it was difficult to ignore the culture and heritage of our surroundings. Amman, situated on a hilly location between the arid desert and the fertile Jordan valley, is a fascinating blend of old and new. The contrast between ancient and contemporary worlds has inspired the poetic epithet, 'a city built on the sands of time'. Much to my disappointment, Paul was unable to describe any of Amman's beauty and historic intrigue as it remained firmly beyond the doors of its city airport. The arrival of so many visitors appeared to throw Jordanian officials into confusion and the only entertainment they could conjure up was an endless tour of airport facilities. In between the repetitive march was a series of brief stops where, once again, we underwent the boring process of being herded into little groups. No doubt the process was merely a ploy to keep us occupied until they could figure out what to do. After what seemed an eternity, we finally boarded a plane bound for Aqaba. The fact that our private jet belonged to King Hussein went a long way towards smoothing the ruffled feathers of travel fatigue and we settled back to enjoy the flight.

Set on the shores of the Red Sea, Aqaba is known to many as the Riviera of Jordan. According to travel literature, it's steeped in culture and is a fantastic place that manages to combine historic sites with an endless variety of high class restaurants, music festivals, and shops. Several of the guides waxed lyrical about the warmth of the Gulf waters, its spectacular coral reefs and the myriad brilliantly coloured fish that live among them. I didn't mind the local fish population but there were a few strange beasties, like sea snakes, stone fish and sharks, that I did my best to avoid. Paul's description of the majestic mountains and how they appeared to change colour with each rising and setting of the sun filled my mind with breathtaking images. These scenic delights may have escaped my visual capability but the sounds and smells of local markets set my other senses racing and proved an intoxicating experience.

Our arrival in Jordan coincided with King Hussein's political agenda in America and prevented him from greeting us in person. After a long bout of serious illness that required him to endure the rigours of chemotherapy, I was amazed at the king's determination to participate in the current peace process, never mind host the European, African and Middle East Championships. Nevertheless, the presence of several members of the royal family at our hotel ensured the highest standard of hospitality as well as an intense level of security. Morale among team members was high as we talked excitedly about the forthcoming competition. Naturally there was a lot of speculation about the kind of boat that would be provided and, when some of the sighted skiers reported they had seen a helicopter deliver a brand new one, we assumed that a Mastercraft had been laid on especially for the tournament. As it turned out, my friends had merely witnessed the arrival of the prince's private boat. Our delusion of grandeur rapidly vanished at the sight of the two ancient tubs waiting for us. Neither would have won prizes for looks but it wouldn't have been so bad if they had been mechanically sound. To our disappointment both gave up the ghost and failed to make it through the practice session. Fortunately some of the coaches and officials were able to strip one of the crafts and find enough mechanical parts to make a single boat work long enough to get us through the competition. It wasn't an ideal situation but we were all grateful for the effort and hard work on our behalf.

Florida's sunshine and humid atmosphere had introduced me to a climate we in Northern Ireland could only imagine, but temperatures in the Middle East literally left me gasping. Swimming in the Gulf waters may be an idyllic experience but, for me, skiing was more of a challenge. The high content of salt in the water made the skis too buoyant and difficult to control, while the backwash from passing oil tankers and pleasure craft had me bobbing around like a cork. Without doubt, as a tourist, I found Jordan fascinating, but as a skier it was incredibly hard work. Apart from soaring temperatures, the unusual mineral content in the water and constant traffic, we had to cope with local curiosity. Very often, play was brought to a complete standstill by sightseers eager to get a closer look at the tournaments. On one occasion, a few got too close for comfort and almost lost their heads. The incident occurred at the end of my second pass in the wake slalom final. Oblivious to everything except completing the course, I was completely flabbergasted when I heard a series of short rapid blasts on the whistle. I'd no idea what was wrong but I knew that Paul was giving me the emergency abort signal and, without hesitation, I let go of the rope and threw myself backwards into the water. It was only later that I realised how close we'd come to tragedy. Apparently, three snorkel divers had surfaced in a triangle directly in my path. Unable to see them, I'd skied straight through, missing them by inches. As Paul led me back to our hotel, I was shaking uncontrollably, horrified by what might have happened. To the onlooker, skiing along the water's surface may look incredibly smooth and innocent but a slalom fin travelling at high speed can decapitate anyone who gets in its way. I don't think the individuals concerned realised they'd had such a lucky escape.

Despite the various setbacks I was happy not only to achieve a silver medal for my slalom performance and a bronze for tricks, but also to set two new Irish records. I learned a lot from the tournament which, apart from testing me to the limit, enabled me to improve my overall scores on the previous season.

When we weren't practising or competing, we all enjoyed the hospitality and generosity of dining with the royal family. Known to King Hussein's son, Prince Abdullah, as 'the happy smiling Irish girl', I did my best to show appreciation for some of the more traditional cuisine. Unfortunately, sheep's eyes, a whole roasted goat decorated with sparklers and a selection of sweetmeats didn't tempt my taste buds. While Paul sampled the odd goat chop, I tended to choose the blander though less spectacular option of pasta. By the time we left Jordan, I'd lost a lot of weight but gained a healthy respect for the simple but delicious taste of home cooking and couldn't wait to tuck into an Ulster fry.

With the competition over, stress levels gradually returned to normal. Determined to make the most of our remaining time, Paul and I decided to do a little sightseeing and booked a trip to the ancient city of Petra, one of UNESCO's world heritage sites. It was an awesome place and definitely deserves its reputation as 'the treasure of the ancient world'. Surrounded by impressive mountains, the road into Petra leads through a long, narrow gorge. Its steeply rising sides manage to obliterate most of the sunshine, making it a cool and gloomy journey. But Paul's description of how the gorge suddenly opens into what was once a natural square, flooded with light and revealing the incredible architecture of the Nabataean people, was awesome. His account of the intricately carved façades bathed in a rosy glow of sunlight sounded beautiful. As I ran my hands over the patterns and traced the delicate outlines, I was astounded by the artistic skill of the nomadic people who, thousands of years ago, had settled in Petra and made it their home. The display of architectural genius continued for another few kilometres but the heat within the city was stifling and, despite my appreciation of the site, I was desperate to leave and find some shade. Paul had taken a few pictures to show friends and family but we almost left Petra with a four-legged souvenir when our guide insisted that the horseback ride into the city was not included in the original price and demanded we hand over an additional payment. Fortunately we'd been warned about the unscrupulous practice and Paul decided to teach the guide a lesson. Telling me not to dismount, he handed over the money, grabbed the reins of my horse and proceeded to lead us away. The guide was furious and ran after us, screaming at Paul to give him back his horse. I couldn't help but laugh at the serious note in Paul's voice as he refused, insisting that he had just paid for the animal and we were taking it home. I've no idea what the man made of the foreigners who thought they could simply walk off with a horse, never mind get it on a plane. Maybe he put it down to a touch of sunstroke and a strange Irish custom. Whatever his reasoning, I'm sure the incident made him think twice before trying the same stunt on other visitors.

The award ceremony took place on the final night of our stay in Jordan but it soon transpired that our hosts also had a reason to celebrate. The Prince Regent's announcement during dinner that King Hussein's visit to Washington had been a huge success and everyone could look forward to a peaceful future was a historic moment. Suddenly, the place erupted in a series of cheers, feet stamping, cutlery rattling and whoops of delight. The atmosphere was electric and, although most of the political detail escaped me, I could empathise with the joy of finding a new hope. Just the year before, people in Northern Ireland had witnessed similar scenes at the signing of what, for many, became known as the 'Good Friday Agreement'. As I listened to the happy voices around me I couldn't help but think that, regardless of differences in culture or tradition, everyone understands the language of peace.

The festivities continued long into the night until finally, at 3 a.m., we left to finish packing and prepare to meet our coach an hour later. The bus driver was obviously a man of many talents as he not only drove us to the airport but opened the departure lounge, turned on the lighting and made sure we were all comfortable. When we boarded the plane and discovered he was also our pilot, I was really impressed.

For me, 1998 was a truly memorable year. It was also a significant time for the water-skiing sport in general when the World Council decided to hold Regional and World Championship competitions on alternate years. Altogether there are three world regions, beginning with Panam, which comprises North and South America as well as Canada. Our region fell into the European, African and Middle East classification, while the third is Asia/Australia. Like their able-bodied colleagues, disabled skiers must compete in the relevant National championships, which are held annually, and allow competitors the opportunity to qualify for the Regional level. Skiers also face a classification process where strength, mobility, balance and ability are assessed by a team of officials who determine the appropriate category. As a totally blind skier, I belonged to the v1 class. Other less visually impaired individuals were allocated v2 status. The same identification method was applied across the whole spectrum of physical disabilities, ensuring no-one need lose out on the chance to succeed.

At National and Regional level, disabled skiers compete against each other but by the time we reach the 'Worlds,' teams are much larger, usually fourteen skiers, making the competition stronger and tougher. After the success in Jordan, my mood was buoyant and it didn't seem possible that life could get any better. Paul was as proud as punch at my achievement and encouraged me to perfect both wake slalom and tricks. The only aspect of water-skiing that he considered out of my league was jump and he was adamant that for a blind person to attempt such a discipline was foolhardy and madness. He was quite vocal on the subject and, to be fair, most experts shared his view that, without vision, jumping a ski ramp was incredibly dangerous. Over the years, I'd learned to trust Paul's judgement in many aspects of my life. I'd come to rely on his candid reply when asked the dreaded question, 'Does my derrière look big in this?' Occasionally, when it came to fashion or home décor, male logic got in the way of his artistic appreciation and forced me to get a second opinion from Mum or one of my female friends. But when it came to water-skiing, there was no-one I trusted more than Paul. He was a professional who had my best interests at heart and I knew that if he categorically refused to let me jump, I had to accept his decision. Yet, my genes for stubbornness and determination are incredibly strong. I should have known that my brain would eventually translate the word 'can't' into 'must'. The precedent had already been set when, in the early days of blindness, Pop insisted I use a conventional cooker because a hob was much too dangerous. Not only did I buy the offending item and conquer it but soon progressed to its much more threatening relation, the range!

While I had no intention of disobeying my husband, an invitation to attend a course in London for visually impaired skiers put temptation in my way. Paul, busy with work, was unable to accompany me for the week-long visit but, as my cane and I made a formidable twosome, I booked the flight and set off. It was an exciting prospect as we were about to sample the latest in water-ski technology. With the aid of an audio slalom system, we could learn to complete the slalom run just like any sighted skier. I was fascinated by the whole event. When I arrived, I met up with many of the European skiers and we bonded immediately. However, on the second day, the guys began teasing me about learning to jump. Naturally, I ignored the implication that I 'couldn't' rather than 'wouldn't' be able to pull it off and refused to rise to the bait. Yet, as the good-natured banter continued, I seriously began to consider the possibility that I might be capable of achieving success. I can only imagine the expression on my friends' faces when I agreed to give it a go. But the silence spoke volumes! They were utterly flabbergasted at the idea I'd actually attempt to jump. It was amazing how, once I'd taken up their challenge, everyone began to backtrack. Nevertheless, I was determined to give it a shot. Perhaps the fact that we were at Heron Lake in London, which is the British National Disabled Water-Ski Centre, with some of the best trainers in the world, provided an added incentive. If I was going to learn to jump, then there was no safer place.

As I stood at the end of the dock and pulled on the jump helmet, bravado fled and I was absolutely petrified. My guide, John Valentine, did his best to reassure me but no matter what he said, my knees continued to knock. In wake slalom and tricks I ski independently, but for the jump discipline it's essential to have a guide ski alongside. Initially John took me round the lake to let me get a feel for the course but the second lap was the real deal. My knuckles must have been white from the strength of my grip on the rope as I listened for the countdown to begin. Five, four, three, two, one, ramp, knees, trees and freeze was the magic formula to get me safely on the other side. Basically the rhyme is an easy way to remember to bend my knees, keep my head up as though searching for tree tops and freeze my body position. As John counted me down, he pulled away to ski behind the boat while I hit the ramp and sailed smoothly over the top. Incredibly, I landed safely on both skis, although I was so shocked, I inadvertently let go of the rope. Keith Knocks, the coach at Heron Lake, was watching from the boat and was delighted by my attempt. After we'd had a brief chat, I decided to try again. Once again I not only landed upright in the water but held firmly onto the rope. It was unbelievable as coaches, guides and other skiers began cheering and clapping. I was so excited that, on my first attempt, I'd been able to make a successful jump.

For the rest of the week, I concentrated on getting to grips with the new audio technology, but at every opportunity I was out on the water practising my jump. I was hooked on it. I desperately wanted to share my latest achievement but there was no way I could tell Paul. Careering round a lake and taking a jump at high speed demands a certain amount of courage but telling my husband what I'd been up to required nerves of steel. I decided that, for the foreseeable future, it should remain my little secret. Things were eventually taken out of my hands when, on the last evening of the trip, Paul happened to ring while my ski buddies and I were in the middle of partying. To my horror they began a teasing chant of 'jumping Jan', unaware that Paul could hear every word and was astute enough to know exactly what had been going on. The silence at the other end of the line was deafening but, like the calm before a storm, it was merely a temporary lull and Paul eventually let rip. For the first time in our married life, I was glad we were on different sides of the Irish Sea.

Back in Belfast, Paul met me at the airport and I could sense his mood immediately. He was still far from friendly. I decided to say as little as possible and let the latest rant run its course. Although when he opened the car boot, pulled out a brand new jump suit and threw it at me, saying, 'Don't ever let me catch you jumping without wearing this,' I knew he'd forgiven me.

A few days later I discovered that, underneath his anger, Paul was secretly delighted by my achievement. He may not have said a lot but the fact that he'd ordered me a pair of jump skis gave the game away.

Chapter 9
World Champion

In August 1999, it seemed that Mother Nature couldn't quite decide her mood. When she wasn't throwing a tantrum and creating havoc with earthquakes, she was playing celestial tricks by using the moon to hide the sun. As the last total eclipse visible from the UK took place on 29 June 1927, long before my birth, I'd never witnessed the spectacular event. Normally I rely on Paul for descriptive input but as the next heavenly scene isn't due until 2090, I'm unlikely to get a first-hand account!

After my delight at learning to jump at London's Heron Lake, I didn't have too long to wait for another episode in what was fast becoming a series of thrilling events. In fact, just five weeks later I was back at Heron Lake, ready to take part in the prestigious 1999 World Disabled Championships. Water-skiing is not an Olympic sport but, as far as skiers are concerned, competing at World level is the pinnacle of achievement. I'd spent the intervening weeks training hard at Cork and felt in great physical shape. Naturally, there was the usual bout of competition nerves, especially as it was the first time I was taking part in all three disciplines: wake slalom, tricks and jumps. Participation in all of the events ensured an opportunity to win the 'big' title of Overall World Champion. This is the dream of every disabled skier. Still a relative newcomer to the sport, I had few expectations and merely hoped to get a respectable result that would avoid any personal embarrassment and take me through to the finals.

By Sunday evening, all the teams had arrived at the hotel, ready for Monday's registration and classification. Tuesday and Wednesday were set aside to allow competitors time to become familiar with the layout of the lake, the length of the run-in for each discipline and the wake of the boat. The opening ceremony got under way on Wednesday evening with an international parade. Dressed in official track suits and carrying their national flags, competitoɪ proudly marched in alphabetical order, representing their respective countries. It was a beautiful summer evening and the air was filled with a heady mixture of floral scent and expectation. Towards the end of the ceremony, Olympic swimmer Sharon Davies presented each of us with a lovely medal to commemorate the event. I'd always admired Sharon and was thrilled to meet her in person. Finally, after officials and skiers had taken the Olympic oath, the championships were declared open and the real party began. With lots of good food, and great company, we had all the ingredients for a fabulous time. Toasting each other's success, we laughed and danced our way through the night.

On my first event, wake slalom, things couldn't have gone better. In fact, I not only went through to the final but set a new Irish record. My level of excitement cranked up a few gears but I still wasn't overly hopeful of achieving major success. The next discipline and my least favourite was tricks. But experience had taught me that the worst thing to do was panic and I was determined to keep my cool and focus. It must have paid off because, later, when I stood on the dock listening to the results, I heard the amazing announcement that Janet Gray from Ireland had won and set a new world record. I was once again through to the finals. It felt so surreal, I was speechless.

Jump was my third and final event. I'd already satisfied a panel of experts as to my competency to enter the jump discipline and the ramp was familiar to me, so I wasn't too nervous. In competition, it's up to the skiers to decide their preferred speed and height. But there are some established rules. Women must jump between a minimum of 1 metre and a maximum of 1.5 metres, while men are not permitted to go any higher than 1.65. For ladies, the top speed is 54 kph but their male counterparts can travel an additional 3 kph, reaching 57 kph. To my surprise, I again performed well and went into the final with a new Irish record as well as one for personal best. It was unbelievable; I was not only competing in the finals but had set my first world record. Despite my happiness, I refused to get too hopeful. There was still another preliminary to come.

Wake slalom was due to be phased out the following year and replaced by the new discipline of audio slalom. As an introduction to the latest in water-ski technology, visually impaired and blind skiers were treated to a demonstration. Although it was a medal event, the results of the audio slalom would not be included in the overall title. Like the other skiers, I was struggling to get to grips with the audio version so didn't expect to do well. Yet, I was already through to the final and was more than happy with my previous performances so I decided to go for it without undue worry. Again I won the prelim with a new Irish record, qualifying for the fourth final. It was a great achievement but, with the finals still to come, I couldn't rest on my laurels or take anything for granted.

The finals began at 7.30 a.m. on Saturday and I was first on the list for wake slalom. As we were running a little behind schedule, I just about managed to get my wet suit on and, in place of a warm-up exercise, I sprinted to the dock. Being late did have its advantages as I didn't have time to think about nerves! Out on the water, the weather was in my favour and as I skied around the course, the surface of the lake was a glassy calm and I knew I'd done well. Back on the dock again, my guide Barry was equally happy but we had to wait to see how the other competitors performed. It seemed ages before the commentator announced that Janet Gray was the new Ladies Wake Slalom World Champion. Wow! What a moment. Not only had I won but I'd set a new European record! It was incredible but with three more finals still to go, there wasn't a lot of time to think about what I'd accomplished.

Winning audio slalom was unbelievable. It was like being in a dream and I didn't want to wake up. Nevertheless, there was still the final for tricks and jumps. The first, tricks, took place after lunch but I have to admit, I was too excited to have much of an appetite. As it turned out, the event went well and I managed to take a silver medal, while an Italian girl, Suzanna Prada, won the gold. Suzie and I shook hands and congratulated one another on our success. I had beaten Suzie in prelims but she won in the final.

On the Sunday morning as I sat on the grass and literally roasted in my jump suit, I'm not sure who was more nervous, my guide Barry or me. Jump was looming and although I'd cleared the same ramp at 1 metre, world champion level demanded I jump 1.25 metres. I tried to focus on the positive aspects. The most important was the calm weather. Thankfully there was no wind. A head wind may give a skier more float in the air but one coming from behind is extremely dangerous as, instead of giving distance as I'd once imagined, it can actually cause the skier to land on their head. Despite landing my first two jumps, inaccurate boat readings meant I had to take mandatory re-runs and by the time I got to the last jump, I was really beginning to tire. In order to get more distance it was necessary to increase speed, something I hadn't done before. Still, I just gritted my teeth, summoned the last remaining ounce of energy, and hoped for the best. Unfortunately, although my landing was fine, I couldn't quite manage to hold onto the rope. This error cost me a gold medal yet, at just nine inches behind the winner, I still walked away with silver. I had been so close and knew that with practice, I'd be able to achieve a faster speed and more height. It was just a matter of time.

At the end of the competition, there was no doubt as to the overall winner. I had done it! I had won the 'big' one and was now officially a champion. At times I thought I must be dreaming but a quick glance at my three gold medals and two silver ones provided sufficient reassurance. I had come to Heron Lake with no expectations and left with three coveted World Champion titles, a world record as well as a host of European and Irish records. It seemed miraculous that out of 118 competitors, I had the highest overall scores. An added bonus was the fact that I had not only won the last of the old wake slalom but the first world audio event.

Paul, unable to be with me at Heron Lake, was following my every movement at home. I'd called him every night but as soon as I knew I'd won the overall title, I rushed to the phone, eager to share the news and unable to contain my happiness. He was ecstatic but by the sound of things, there was more than my husband celebrating my victory. Apparently he was playing host to twelve Irish wake boarders who'd travelled throughout Ireland to take part in various competitions. Their arrival at our club Meteor had coincided with my debut at 'Worlds' and Paul had invited them to share in the excitement and help him celebrate.

The awards ceremony at Heron was fantastic. When I went forward to receive my medals, the crowd went crazy. The sound of stamping feet, clapping hands and whistles filled my ears. It was wonderful. I was the new girl and I'd certainly created a bit of a storm. I'd also made a lot of new friends among the disabled skiing community and had enjoyed a lot of fun. As I walked back to my place, I felt jubilant. Who would have believed that, in a relatively short time, I could have accomplished so much?

The next day, I returned to Cork with the rest of the Irish team. Totally exhausted and emotionally drained, I was ready for nothing more exciting than a hot bath and a long sleep. But Paul had other ideas. When I arrived at my coach's house and my husband opened the door, I was flabbergasted. Determined to be the first to offer his congratulations, the poor man had driven the seven-hour journey from Belfast to Cork and proved he was my number one fan. At the sound of his familiar voice, tiredness vanished and I was overwhelmed with happiness as we headed off to enjoy a champagne breakfast. Any hope of a snooze later in the day had to be postponed when I was inundated with a barrage of interview requests from local television and radio stations. Suddenly, the title of World Water-ski Champion had turned me into a celebrity and I was hot news. It was a little disconcerting but once I got chatting I found I really enjoyed it.

Once back in Belfast, the attention continued and I seemed to spend most of my time in a radio or television studio. It was great fun. Winning at the 'Worlds' had triggered a burst of adrenaline that kept me on a continual high, but as normality began to kick in, I realised just how much the competitions had taken out of me. Training for the event had proved a punishing schedule and I decided that my body deserved a rest. However, an unexpected phone call almost extended the two-week break from skiing indefinitely. When the BBC invited me to come on board as a researcher at Belfast's Broadcasting House, I was flattered as well as stunned. Despite having completed a short course in media studies, I'd never envisaged a role within such a prestigious company. I have to admit it was a tempting offer. Yet, I'd just won the 'Worlds' and I wasn't sure a change of career at this stage was what I wanted. After talking it over with Paul, I decided that when it came to a choice between water-skiing and working in an office, albeit doing an interesting job, there really wasn't any choice. I was a natural water baby. I loved skiing and had just been declared the best in the world. I'd reached the top, but Paul and I knew how hard I'd have to work if I wanted to stay there. Working with the BBC was indeed a great opportunity, but if I wanted to take my sport seriously, I had no option but to decline.

Paul's interest in wake boarding, a sport that's a bit like snow boarding except it takes place on the water, had developed rapidly and, as well as competing, he was also a qualified judge. Very often, Toyah and I accompanied him to competitions and, while my tiny canine chum barked her encouragement from the boat, I too would take part in the events. My inability to see the wake put me at a major disadvantage to sighted boarders but my experience with tricks came in handy, helping me pull up a few points with various impressive little rotations. New boarders, amazed by my ability, would often ask how I managed to do so well. They were all given the standard reply that I was sleeping with the chief judge, although I usually waited a while before confessing I was actually married to him. In an effort to be even-handed, Paul marked me fairly hard and some of the other officials on the panel jokingly commented that I was sleeping with the wrong judge.

The finals of the wake boarding competition were held at the end of September at Still Waters WSC in Naas, just outside Dublin. I'd already competed in 'Rookie' category in most of the four stops and was looking forward to the final event. Wake boarding was good competition experience and I loved meeting up with all the other boarders. To my delight I won the final tour, making me Irish Rookie Board Tour Champion. It was the perfect end to the skiing season. However, the incident that proved the icing on the cake and touched me greatly had nothing to do with winning titles. It occurred when a waitress in our hotel dining room recognised me and came rushing over to give me an emotional hug. Before I knew what was happening the poor woman was sobbing out her story. Apparently, her husband had been suffering from severe clinical depression and refused to get medical help. His sombre moods had not only made him miserable but thrown his family into utter despair. The woman went on to explain how her son had seen the national news coverage of my triumphant return from the World Championships and insisted his dad watch the next bulletin. To the family's amazement, the man, after witnessing how I'd been able to overcome blindness and achieve so much, broke down and agreed to get help for his problem. It was the first time I realised that my success could be an inspiration to others. I was really moved by the stranger's story and decided to send her husband a present. On the back of one of my photos, I wrote 'The only way is up'. It was a message that I too had had to learn.

The skiing season ended on a real high but I knew there was a lot of hard training ahead. My nomination for the Belfast Telegraph Sports Award provided an opportunity to indulge in a bit of retail therapy and when I learned that I'd won for the second time, I was over the moon.

Champion boxer Wayne McCullough presented my award but it was later in the evening when we got chatting and discovered that, although we'd never met before, our grandmothers had been friends for many years. It is such a small world. That night, on a cloud of happiness, I took home more than great memories and a trophy from the Belfast Telegraph. I also had Wayne's offer to teach me how to throw a perfect left hook, just in case my coach ever got too big for his ski boots!

Chapter 10
The Millennium

On 31 December 1999, it seemed that the whole world was holding its breath in anticipation of a new era. Although, with a calendar that's influenced by the astronomic calculations of ancient Egypt and over seven years behind its Gregorian counterpart, Ethiopia may have found the Millennium celebrations a little premature.

For the rest of us, the countdown had begun long before the stroke of midnight on New Year's Eve. In fact, preparations for the musical extravaganza and fireworks displays, not to mention London's Millennium Dome, had been the subject of discussion for an indeterminate and lengthy amount of time. Finally, the moment had arrived. In a few seconds, the clock would usher in, not only another year but a new millennium. Paul and I, like most of Belfast's inhabitants, had planned to join our friends in the city centre to soak up the atmosphere, say goodbye to the old year and christen the next with a chorus of Auld Lang Syne and a glass of champagne. But, as experience had taught me, nothing ever goes according to plan. The only things Paul and I managed as 1999 slipped into history and a new age began, were a few croaky words of mutual sympathy, a couple of painkillers and a swig of cough medicine. Unfortunately we both came down with a bout of flu and spent the party season safely and soberly tucked up in bed. I was really disappointed as I'd been looking forward to Belfast's biggest ever celebration. Still, there was always Ethiopia's Millennium in 2007!

Thankfully by the end of January we were fighting fit and within a short space of time had not only moved Paul's electronic business to the Gas Works complex in Belfast, but bought a new home on the outskirts of Lisburn. I was sad to leave our old place as it held so many good memories. It was on the hilly streets of Belfast's Cavehill that my white cane and I had developed a trusting relationship, allowing me an unprecedented amount of freedom. Paul and I had also made a lot of lovely friends whose kindness and ready acceptance made our time there so special. But, as water-skiing was now a full-time career, it made life a lot easier to live within easy commuting distance of Lough Henney. However, for me, the rural location initially posed a few obstacles. With no public transport, travelling to the nearest village or the centre of Lisburn was a bit of a problem. Determined to find a solution, I decided I'd better get to know the drivers at the local taxi firm! I think, if he was honest, Paul would have to admit he was secretly pleased that my spontaneous shopping trips had come to an end. No more hopping on a bus at the end of the road and heading to town for a bit of retail therapy. In future any desire for a spending spree would be tempered by the rigmarole of having to plan everything in advance.

Changing address had in the past proved an ordeal that triggered an avalanche of apprehension and fear. This current move, if not entirely worry-free, was much less traumatic. However, I did occasionally succumb to a few moments of panic! After all, apart from the restrictions of a rural location, I was leaving behind a whole network of

Janet on a visit to Phoenix Park, Dublin, with Granda Billy, 1965.

Janet aged three, with baby fawn,
Phoenix Park, 1965.

Janet aged four, with deer, Phoenix Park, 1966.

School photo, aged five.

Janet, Ian and Pop on holiday, 1970. Point of Ayre lighthouse in the Isle of Man.

Janet and Ian at the funfair, Isle of Man, 1971.

Ian, Granny Snowdon, Janet, Mum and Pop. Peel Castle, Isle of Man, 1972.

School photo, aged ten.

Paul and Janet's wedding day, 11 August 1984, Sinclair Seamen's Presbyterian Church, Belfast.

Janet and pet poodle Toyah, Mum, Pop and Ian. Glenarrif Forest Park, Glens of Antrim, 1986.

The family celebrates Janet's Most Excellent Order of the British Empire award, New Year's Honours, 2002.

Janet receives her MBE from HRH Prince Charles at Buckingham Palace, February 2002.

Janet meets Eamonn Holmes
at the Irish Tatler Women of
the Year Awards, Dublin, 2002.

Team GB. World Disabled Water-Ski Championships, 2003, Florida.

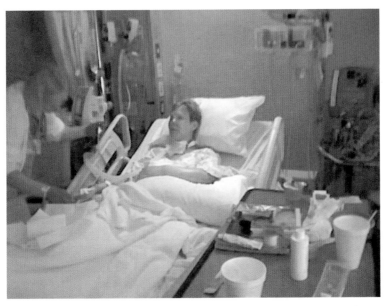

Janet on life support in Tampa General Hospital's ICU, just after the accident in March 2004.

Janet receives an honorary doctorate from Queen's University Belfast, July 2004.

An overhead shot of slalom training in Florida, February 2008.

Slalom training in Florida, 2008.

Janet tricking and waving to crowds at River Fest, Coleraine, June 2008.

Janet and the twins, Hollie and Harvey, in the ski boat at Meteor Water-Ski Club, Lough Henney, 2009.

Children from Maghaberry Primary School who did the Disability Sports five-star challenge as part of Janet's Freedom of the City celebrations, 18 April 2009.

Paul and Janet are driven by horse and carriage through the streets of Lisburn on Janet's conferment as Freeman of the City of Lisburn.

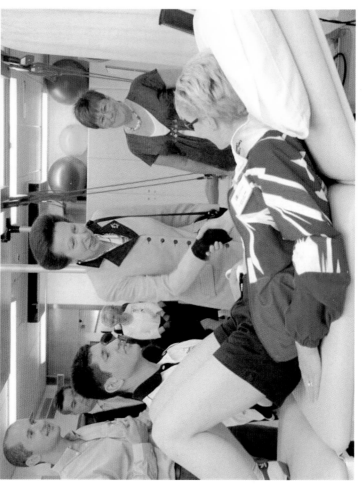

Janet meets HRH Princess Anne at the University of Ulster, Jordanstown, High Performance Sports Centre, 2009.

support from friends and family. Nevertheless, any irrational concerns were transient and usually passed fairly quickly. I was no longer the same frightened girl who had allowed glaucoma to rob her of independence and joy. I had developed into a mature and confident woman, who, despite the challenges of being blind, had discovered an unquenchable passion and zest for life. Instead of feeling 'odd' or 'different' to my contemporaries, I was finally the happy, carefree and independent person that I always knew was the real me. Like many couples who embark on an adventure by moving outside their comfort zone, Paul and I adopted a pragmatic attitude. Instead of fretting over potential problems, we decided to enjoy the experience and, if we didn't like life in the countryside, we could always up sticks and move back to Belfast. The one most affected by the move was my little doggie friend, Toyah. Over the years, the toy poodle had been my constant companion but her gradual loss of sight and eventual blindness left her disorientated and afraid of unfamiliar environments. The move to Lisburn caused the poor thing a lot of stress. My heart went out to her as I certainly understood her feelings. Still, with a lot of kisses and reassurance Toyah settled down and began to enjoy her new surroundings as much as I did. The house proved much larger than the previous one at Cavehill but instead of anxiety, I felt a tremor of excitement as I eagerly explored, feeling my way around and rapidly getting to grips with the layout. With three levels to decorate and furnish, I enjoyed, much to Paul's concern, a full quota of shopping trips.

By this stage, my remaining senses had greatly compensated for lack of vision, allowing me to comprehend my relation to the outside world. My fingertips could trace the most intricate patterns and relay an extremely accurate image to my brain, while a heightened sense of hearing allowed me to detect even the smallest sound. The ability to 'see' what's going on has, over the years, provided me with a

few funny anecdotes. On one occasion, Paul and I were
entertaining friends when I heard him momentarily leave the
room. As well as the sound of the door opening and closing,
I detected the noise that his glass made as he set it on our
little tiled coffee table. However, no-one else had noticed.
When he came back, forgetting where he'd placed his drink,
he asked if anyone had seen it. Our friends were
flabbergasted when I calmly turned in his direction and said,
'It's on the coffee table, where you left it!' On the other hand,
my acute hearing can sometimes lead to a row when I catch
every muttered word that Paul thinks is out of range.
Sometimes, he'll tease me by lightly touching my lips and
moving quickly away, but he rarely manages to move fast
enough and, after fair warning that I'm getting annoyed, he
usually ends up getting his finger bitten! On a more serious
note, my auditory ability has helped save a life. The incident
occurred during a swimming session when a young woman
suffered an epileptic seizure while still in the water. Her cry
wasn't loud. In fact it seemed little more than a faint yelp of
shock, but thank God I heard it and was able to swim in her
direction and pull her to safety. I'm still not certain that, if I'd
been sighted, my hearing would have been sufficiently
developed to pick up on her note of distress.

While other senses have, to a certain degree, made up for
my inability to see, there are some scenarios where sight is
essential. Regardless of how sensitive or developed, it is
almost impossible to distinguish the seedier side of human
nature by hearing or touch. On many occasions, I have, like
other visually challenged people, been robbed by those in a
position of trust. Disappointed and hurt, even by those we
counted as friends, I've also lost count of the number of
times I've been the target of unscrupulous taxi drivers who
have taken £20 for what should have been a £5 fare. Unable to
see, I trustingly offered the note only to find on my return
home, I'd been cheated. Yet, to be fair, I am unable to count

the numerous acts of kindness shown to me. On the whole, it seems that there is more good than bad in the world and my local taxi firm must have the politest, most generous drivers in the region. These days, experience has taught me to minimise the potential for loss and I always know the exact contents of my purse!

Just a week after we'd moved to the Lisburn area, I was off for an intensive training session in Cork. With no flights to the region, Paul left me at the train station in Belfast where I began the first leg of a long and solitary journey. Once I'd arrived in Dublin, I had to take a taxi to the next station which, with all my ski equipment plus a suitcase, was not an easy feat. Very often cab drivers, after spotting the huge amount of luggage, would take to the road at an incredible speed and leave me standing open-mouthed and furious. After a while, and several missed connections that added yet another few hours to the trip, I learned it was better to book a taxi in advance. But no matter how well planned, the eight-hour excursion was both lonely and exhausting. As a three event skier, I had to take a bag big enough to contain the various skis. At 8 ft long with wheels at one end, my baggage took on the proportions of an oversized coffin. In fact, when asked by a curious guard what was in the bag, I couldn't resist the retort, 'Granny!'

The frequent trips soon began to take their toll and, as they became more physically draining, I knew it was time to find another, more accessible location to train. At a mere fifteen minutes drive from Heathrow airport, Heron Lake in Wraysbury seemed a perfect solution. With accommodation on site, the centre would not only provide me with the means for intensive training sessions, but also a high degree of much-valued independence. I was really excited to begin practice for the 2000 European competitions but almost as soon as I arrived at Heron Lake, my luck took a bit of a nosedive. Unfortunately, during jump I landed badly, tearing the tendons and injuring the muscles in my arm. There was nothing else for it but to return home and undergo a few gruelling weeks of physiotherapy.

Returning to Belfast may have been disappointing but it shouldn't have been difficult. All I had to do was get to the airport and allow staff to lead me on board the plane. Everything appeared to be going to plan until, seated comfortably in the aircraft, I happened to notice I was surrounded by an extraordinary amount of Scottish accents. Initially, I assumed that Northern Ireland must be having an influx of Celtic visitors. When the chap next to me enquired if I was glad to be going home, I replied that, once we arrived in *Belfast* I didn't have far to go. Immediately he picked up on the emphasis of my destination and responded, 'Don't you mean you're going to Edinburgh?' With that, I unclipped my seat belt, pressed the cabin crew alert and announced to the astonished passengers that I was on the wrong flight. Apparently, the airport staff had mistakenly led me through the gate for an imminent departure to Scotland. Thankfully, the flight to Belfast waited for me to be transferred and to the sound of good-natured clapping and cheering, I took my seat. Settling back in my chair, I soon forgot any embarrassment at causing a delay and began to relax. Closing my eyes, I prepared to take a quick nap and dream about spending the evening with Paul and our little dog, Toyah. Being with my husband and our tiny pet was the highlight of my life and I missed them dreadfully. However, as usual, fate intervened and altered my plans. Ironically, as the plane approached Belfast airport, the pilot made an interesting announcement. Due to bad weather and thunderstorms, he was unable to land as scheduled and would have to divert to another destination. Guess where? Glasgow! The plane was in an uproar as everyone laughingly blamed me for the diversion. It seems I was destined to spend the night in Scotland.

The injury to my arm meant a daily trip to the physiotherapist but, to my disappointment, it also excluded me from the European competitions. Like me, my colleague Eamonn, the other half of the Irish team, was equally short on luck. The poor guy was put out of action when he broke his leg during a training exercise. I've no idea what fate was playing at but we were obviously the target for a bit of mischievous sport.

As the Millennium drew to a close, I thought that, despite the unlucky streak, the year hadn't turned out too badly. At the Irish National Championships held at Muckno wsc, I not only took gold in all three disciplines but set a new Irish record in audio slalom. I was delighted to return home with gold overall and the title of Irish Ladies Champion. The fact that I had competed against able-bodied skiers added to my sense of achievement.

As a hobby, water-skiing is a great way to have fun, get out in the fresh air and clear the mind. But as a career, the sport demands optimum levels of strength and stamina. Like all full-time skiers, I spend a lot of time working out in the gym. I have to admit that I'm extremely fortunate that our local council is very supportive of its athletes and has allowed me to use the facilities at Lisburn's state of the art Leisure Plex, completely free of charge. The instructors, a lovely group and all very helpful, have, no doubt, found me frustrating as I tended to exercise my tongue more than any other muscle. I seemed to have an aversion to working up a sweat and getting hot and sticky. In fact I've always tried to do as little as possible in the gym. But what I avoided on the treadmill, I more than made up for in the pool or out on the lake. Instead of exercise, I regarded swimming as a pleasure and would happily spend hours in the water. With so much time spent at the gym, I'd made a lot of friends and was delighted to be nominated for the Lisburn Sports Awards. As runner-up in the event, I felt it a great honour.

There's no doubt that the year 2000 brought its fair share of excitement and rewards. But already attention was turning to the next big event, the 2001 World Championships. Due to be held in Melbourne, Australia, I knew this competition would pose a whole different set of challenges. For a start, as it was scheduled to take place in March, at a time when our home season hadn't even started, I had to find a warmer climate to begin some serious training. Paul and I began to research some winter ski schools and discovered McCormick's, in Tampa, Florida. As well as being an establishment for professional skiers, their website promised on site accommodation, which for me proved the deciding factor.

Once again, my cane and I were off on our travels. The baggage, as usual, was heavy and cumbersome but I managed to get from Belfast to Tampa with both equipment and me in one piece. The sun on my face made a lovely change to the sleety rain I'd left behind in Lisburn and I looked forward to getting settled into my temporary residence and finding my way down to the dock. That was my first big shock. The 'accommodation' turned out to be nothing more than a wooden hut. Apparently the school building was still under construction and I had to make do with what was available. Feeling my way around, I realised that I had been allocated approximately 3 metres x 3 metres of living space, a set of rickety bunk-beds, drawers to match and a television. I could only thank God that I couldn't 'see' the state of the bathroom! Once I'd got over the shock at the lack of facilities, I decided to make my way towards the dock. As I suspected, that too caused a dilemma. There was no way I could haul equipment back and forth on a daily basis, I'd be too wrecked to ski. The solution was simple and obvious. All I had to do was leave the gear at a particular spot on the covered dock so I would know where to find it. Food wasn't a problem as school dinners were included in the price. For five days every week, we commenced training at 7.30 a.m., broke for lunch at noon and then continued until 6 p.m. Saturday was a half day session while Sunday was strictly R&R. It was a hard slog and I missed the comforts of home but I really enjoyed the warm Florida sunshine. I couldn't wait to get back to my nice comfy bed but it would be hard to get used to the cold damp Northern Irish weather, never mind the chilly waters of Lough Henney.

With the prospect of visiting Australia and the opportunity to compete in the 'Worlds', I ignored the discomfort of cramped conditions and knuckled down to make sure I was the best I could possibly be. By the time I left Florida, I was ready. I was going to Australia and I was determined to win. Blindness had long since taken a back seat in my journey through life. It no longer played a dominant role. I was about to go on the biggest adventure of my life and I couldn't wait.

Chapter 11

Down Under

I'm not sure what I expected to find in Australia. Like the early European settlers of the 1800s, I hoped it would be a lot of gold! With approximately four million inhabitants, Melbourne is a thriving metropolis, enjoying a reputation as the sporting and cultural capital of Australia. Competing in any world championship is always a thrilling experience but when it means travelling to the other side of the world, there's a whole new element of excitement.

I couldn't wait for the adventure to begin. By this stage, I was well used to getting on and off planes with only my cane and airport staff to help. But on this occasion, I was relieved and happy that I was being accompanied by my team-mate Eamonn, his dad John, who was also our team captain, and his sister Sinéad, who acted as my guide. I knew Paul would have loved to come too but there was no way he could leave his business commitments.

Finally, after weeks of preparation, departure day arrived. Friends and family wished me luck but I knew that, despite my attempts to reassure them, Mum and Pop were worried about my safety. They did their best to hide their anxiety but I could always tell when something was bothering them. It wasn't easy for them to appreciate my need for independence and freedom. Like all parents, especially those with children who suffer from a disability, their natural inclination was to try to protect me, but very often that would have meant clipping my wings.

Our first week in Australia was spent in Sydney, where we spent our time visiting the tourist attractions and soaking up the atmosphere. The following week we flew up to Brisbane where the famous jump coach Ray Stokes helped us prepare for the competition. As well as a fantastic opportunity to take advantage of his professional training, we were all glad to spend a few days acclimatising to our surroundings. Australia, like Florida, was a real treat to the senses. Down by the lake, the sound of unusual birds and wildlife seemed strange and exotic. One morning, as we made our way along a dirt track leading down to the water, John suddenly stopped the jeep to let a lizard pass. For a moment I thought the Aussie air must be bringing out the softer side of our team captain, who apparently couldn't bring himself to squash such a tiny creature. But when he pointed out that it was a monitor lizard that had wandered into our path, I realised the delay wasn't due to an act of Irish kindness. As a member of a species that includes the heaviest living lizard, the Komodo dragon, our reptilian friend was not easily ignored. We had no choice but to stop and allow him right of way. No doubt his reputation as a carnivore helped avoid any desire for an argument.

Within a few days, I began to realise that monitor lizards were actually the least of my worries. Florida's subtropical climate had introduced me to some weird and wonderful species but when it came to variety, there was simply no contest. Australia, home to some of the world's most poisonous creatures, won every time. With python snakes wriggling beneath the surface, I was terrified of falling into the water and made sure I never missed a jump. However, there were worse things than splashing around in a snake-infested lake. As soon as I learned about the nasty habits of 'funnel-web' spiders, I developed a dread of going to the loo. The insect, one of the world's most venomous, loves to hang around toilet bowls waiting to sink its fangs into an unsuspecting bottom. When I could no longer ignore the call of nature, I'd make a great racket by kicking open the door and banging my stick frantically around the walls, hoping the noise would scare the intruders off.

Compared to Brisbane's hot, sticky weather, Melbourne was freezing cold, wet and extremely windy. To make matters worse, I woke up on the morning of the opening ceremony with a thumping headache, aching joints and a soaring temperature. There couldn't have been a worse time, except maybe for the Millennium celebrations, to come down with flu. I was devastated that, instead of enjoying the event, I was confined to bed. It seemed that all my hard work had been in vain and even before I'd started, I was out of the competition. What I needed was a good dose of tender loving care with an added measure of encouragement. A phone call to Paul did the trick and gave me an additional spurt of fight and determination. Summoning up the last vestiges of energy, I told myself that I hadn't flown to the opposite side of the world and battled reptiles and deadly spiders to be beaten by a virus. I may not win, but there was no way I was going home without putting up a fight for my titles. Brave words, but I still felt miserable.

The arrival of my Auntie Marie, Pop's sister, who had flown in from New Zealand to lend her support, soon brought a smile to my face. The appearance of my two cousins, Paul from Adelaide and David from Sydney, added an extra boost to my morale. My family's unexpected presence was just the tonic I needed and I loved having the opportunity to spend time with them. When relatives from Mum's side of the family, who had long since emigrated to

Melbourne, turned up unexpectedly, I was on top of the world. As I took my position on the lake I couldn't help but join in the crowd's laughter when the commentator announced 'next up is Janet Gray from Ireland and it looks as though she's brought half the country with her!'

Normally, a torrential downpour and gale force winds during a competition would have been enough to knock me off my course. At such a prestigious event, the awful storms should have left my knees knocking with fear. Yet, as I stood on the dock, it didn't matter how miserable the weather, a raging temperature was already giving me the chills. I think I was too ill to be nervous. Physically I felt dreadful, yet having my family around really lifted my spirits and made me determined to give it my best shot and make them all proud. As I went out to jump, a strong tail wind began making conditions treacherous but all I could think about was my guide John. I just hoped he'd be okay and not be blown off course. Despite the extreme weather, I managed to land first time before waving to the crowd and skiing off. As I climbed onto the dock, there was an announcement informing skiers that the jump event had been cancelled and those still to compete would have their scores taken from the preliminary round. If only they'd come up with that decision a little earlier, I too could have avoided the jump.

By the time I left Melbourne, I had another collection of gold medals. It was fantastic; I was going home with one for every discipline! I was the overall World Champion, but there's no doubt, between storms and illness, my victory had been a hard-fought battle and the medals well-deserved. Paul couldn't wait for my return but it seemed such a shame to waste an opportunity to spend time with my family. I didn't know how long it would be before we'd be able to meet again and so I decided to stay in Australia for another three weeks and enjoy some quality time with my relatives. It was a wonderful time filled with many trips down memory lane, lots of laughter and a few celebratory toasts to future as well as past success.

Two days before I was due to leave, we decided to visit Queenscliff and swim with wild bottlenose dolphins. After we sailed out to sea, a few dolphins were spotted swimming alongside the boat, and everyone began talking excitedly about how beautiful they were. I'd heard of this experience but as I climbed overboard and slipped into the water I realised I'd no idea what to expect. We didn't have long to wait and before I knew what was happening, I was told we were surrounded by at least six fins; I just hoped we weren't in the middle of a scene from *Jaws*. Gradually more and more dolphins joined us until there were at least thirty of the mammals, swimming beneath us, jumping over our heads and generally having a great deal of fun. Known for their intelligence, they're also amazingly friendly. Touching the gentle creatures, I felt so free and at one with nature. It was great to be alive. Swimming with wild dolphins was an awesome experience and I knew I'd treasure it for ever.

The journey home alone to Belfast was long and tiring but I didn't care. I'd been away for six weeks and I was desperately missing Paul. It was great to be back in our own home with its comfy sofa and, more importantly, spider-free loo! Once again, I was inundated with requests to meet the media and talk about my new titles and stack of medals. But somehow, the only subject on my mind was swimming with the bottlenose dolphins.

With the 'Worlds' out of the way, I intended to spend the home season developing new tricks and improving my slalom technique. Unfortunately, a collision with the door of a bathroom cabinet put me out of action and instead of zooming around the lake I ended up spending the whole summer lying flat on my back in bed. I'd just taken a bath and as I bent to gather up the towels, my eye connected with the partially open door. It was excruciatingly painful but I thought it was relatively minor until Paul took me to hospital and doctors discovered a lot of internal bleeding. Concerned that it could reach my brain, they ordered me to lie flat and allow the blood to drain. It was infuriating that such a small incident could have such major consequences. A few days later, the death of our dog Toyah added to my sadness. The little poodle suffered a stroke and passed peacefully away. It was heartbreaking as I'd had her for so long and she was such a comfort to me. In fact, she was my best friend. For both Paul and I the house seemed very empty without her.

Confined to bed and missing Toyah, life seemed pretty bleak but a letter from Downing Street soon brought a smile to my face. Apparently I'd been recommended to receive a Royal Honour. I couldn't believe my ears and made Paul read it three times to make sure I wasn't dreaming. There was absolutely no doubt; I was about to be made a Member of the Most Excellent Order of the British Empire. It was such an amazing thing to happen and I felt enormously privileged. Of course, the first thing I wanted to do was call my mum and tell her the news but we were sworn to secrecy. Everyone would have to wait until it was announced in the 2002 New Year's Honours List. It was really difficult not to blurt it out but at the same time I loved hugging it to myself. It was such a delicious secret.

By Christmas time, my injury had healed and life had once again resumed its hectic pace. With the cupboards full of seasonal goodies and presents wrapped and under the tree, Paul and I settled down for a relaxing Christmas Eve. Just as we were toasting the season, our friend Max arrived, saying he had a present for me. I'm not sure what I expected, maybe a bottle of perfume or some lovely chocolates. However, I never would have guessed it was a training session with the army. At first I thought it was a joke, especially as Paul and Max rolled about laughing at my expression, but on 6 January, I turned up at the army barracks and reported for duty. Despite my initial shock it really was a thoughtful gift. After the accident, I'd missed out on the ski season and my fitness levels weren't up to standard. As it turned out, the army's instructor was brilliant and really put me through my paces. I'd never worked so hard or sweated so much in my life. In fact, at one point I even considered desertion. Yet, within a short time, I really began to notice an improvement in my strength and stamina. It was sheer hard work but I felt wonderful.

The release of the New Year's Honours List caused great excitement among friends and family. Mum and Pop were thrilled by the prospect of going to Buckingham Palace and delighted that I was to receive an MBE in recognition of my services to disabled sport. Naturally for such a special occasion we had to find a perfect outfit, so Mum and I hit the shops. The search proved more difficult than expected as the January sales were still in full swing and few places had received any new spring stock. But, I never give up! Originally, I hadn't intended to wear black but I was getting desperate. Eventually, I discovered an outfit that Mum assured me was gorgeous and very classy. Fortunately the black suit with white trimming looked great and was easy to accessorise, which saved a whole lot of hassle.

Visiting Buckingham Palace was an incredible experience. Mum and Paul kept up a running commentary, describing everything around us. The décor and paintings sounded very grand and beautiful. As Her Majesty was away on her Golden Jubilee Tour, and unable to present the awards in person, Prince Charles took over the role and was, as all princes should be, utterly charming. While Paul and my parents took their seats among the audience, I was looked after by the Head Butler, a lovely gentleman who kept me entertained with a stream of interesting historical facts. I wasn't at all nervous as we were told what to expect. I found the whole thing fascinating.

My family was so proud to watch me receive the MBE. Prince Charles had obviously been well informed about both me and my sport. When he asked if I was ever frightened going over the jump, I told him that if I could see the thing, I probably wouldn't do it.

The day went perfectly. I had a great time but it ended on a particularly lovely note. After receiving my honour, I had just taken my place beside Paul when the butler whispered that someone was waiting downstairs to see me. Paul led me to what he described as a beautiful grandiose staircase, which sounded fabulous. Yet, it wasn't until I got to the bottom that I discovered the real surprise. There, waiting to be the first to offer her congratulations, was Dame Mary Peters. It was such a considerate thing for her to do. I'd first met Mary in 1974 when, as a young schoolgirl, I took part in the opening event of the Mary Peters Track. Later, we met again through the Ulster Sports Trust and various sporting events. Mary took me under her wing and has been an enormous help throughout my career. We're great friends and I love her to bits.

Unfortunately, by 2002 the Irish WaterSki Federation was falling apart at the seams and with no support structures in place, I was forced to ski for Great Britain. Athletes living in Northern Ireland can choose whom they wish to represent. As our home club, Meteor, was affiliated with the Irish Federation, I skied for Ireland, although I was often approached and invited to join the British team. In the end I had no choice as, if my career was to continue, I had to go along the only route open to me. However, despite the fact that I was merely changing flags and not countries, I had to take a mandatory year out of international competitions. Still, it proved a good time to change, as 2002 was a European year, meaning that I would be able to compete in the 2003 World Championships. Flags may have changed but the sport was still the same and I was doing what I loved best. I looked forward to adding to my rapidly growing collection of gold.

The British Disabled Team coach was based at Whitworth Waterski and Recreation Centre in the Pennines. In the week leading up to the British Disabled National Championships, I trained at the centre, planning to hitch a lift to the competition in Scotland with my team-mate Alan. By the time the poor guy got his wheelchair, two sets of luggage and all our ski equipment into the car, there was barely enough room for us. The drive to the Scottish National Water-Ski Centre in Dunfermline was long and tiring. We couldn't wait to get to our guest house and have a rest. The only problem was that we couldn't find it. Alan decided to drive to a police station and ask for directions. With his chair buried under a mountain of gear, I had to be the one to go into the station and find help. It was hilarious. I got out of the car, cane in hand, and with Alan calling, 'right a bit Janet, turn left, up two steps,' I finally managed to find my way inside.

The policeman on duty must have thought us a strange pair when I asked him to come outside and give my friend directions. But that's a typical example of how we in the disabled community get things done. We pool our resources and do them together.

Paul managed to get a few days off and flew over to join me for the tournament. Just before the competition we had a team meeting and I have to admit that our coach's instruction not to break a world record seemed a bit strange. However, it was simply part of a strategic plan. If we held back until the 2003 Worlds, there was more chance of earning team points and giving the Great Britain team a greater opportunity to take the 'Team Title'.

The lakes at Town Lough are perfectly designed, man-made and make great skiing water. I was happy with my audio slalom, setting a European record in the final. Tricks, on the other hand, was a disaster when I fell in the first round. I couldn't believe I'd made such a simple mistake but I made sure there wasn't a repeat performance, and in the finals I won with a new British record.

Immediately before the jump, my team captain took me aside and once again emphasised the instruction not to break the world record. I agreed to keep the ramp at 1.5 metres but to decrease my speed so that I would simply 'plop' over. I wasn't nervous as I left the dock with my guide Robin, there was no pressure to perform, in fact just the opposite. I did as I agreed and dropped my speed, landing easily on the other side. However, as we came round for number two, we passed the dock area and Robin told me that my score was showing 12.9. I couldn't believe it, the world record was 11.9 metres. I'd unintentionally broken not only the record but my promise! Any hope that Robin's lack of specs had caused him to mis-read the board rapidly vanished when, on the second jump, I scored 13.2 and heard my angry team captain screaming for me to come in immediately. Wow, was I in trouble! Yet, despite Chris our team captain's annoyance with me, the other members clapped and cheered, showing full support. I told Chris to keep his hair on, that when the time was right, I'd simply break the record again. I just hoped I could pull it off. It was my first British Nationals and by winning all four championship titles, I got to take the entire silverware home with me. If I kept this up, we'd need a bigger house!

Chapter 12
Hooked on a Feeling

There's no doubt that winning the title of World Champion is the thrill of a lifetime. In any sport, it is the ultimate goal. For me, reaching the pinnacle of my career provided a fantastic sense of achievement and I was determined to remain at the top and enjoy it for as long as possible. But staying ahead of the competition requires 100 per cent commitment. Once training gets under way there's no time for the more frivolous things in life, like spending time with friends or relaxing in front of the telly. There's definitely no opportunity to go shopping! However, once training is over, I love to unwind, catch up on a bit of girlie gossip and then hit the town for some serious retail therapy. Like many women, I have a weakness for handbags and shoes. Unfortunately, like the majority of men, my husband doesn't share my shopping passion and after an hour is totally fed up with traipsing round the high street. For me, it's a real treat to spend the day with one of my girlfriends who is equally as mad about finding the perfect pair of shoes and matching bag.

As an elite athlete on the Athlete Support Programme with Sports Northern Ireland, I was the perfect candidate for the Sports Institute Northern Ireland, which was created in 2003.

This facility comprises a wide range of experts who offer their knowledge to young athletes who want to reach and stay at the top of their sporting profession. There's advice on everything from nutrition to sport psychology. Strength and conditioning coaches, physiotherapists and sports science officers co-ordinate their skills to ensure that each elite athlete enjoys an individual and tailor-made programme suited to their schedule.

I have to confess that the SINI was a bit of a shock to my system. While disability can occur at any stage in life, those from the disabled water-skiing community tend to have encountered it later in life and, like me, have found sport a great way to rebuild their lives. As a mature athlete, I was used to doing my own thing and found it hard to adjust to the tightly controlled environment. My idea of fitness and diet also came in for a makeover when I learned that, according to SINI experts, elite athletes do not drink mugs of coffee and eat bars of chocolate between training sessions. I was already a world champion and if I wanted to remain one in 2003, I would have to follow their advice.

The World Championship Competitions were held at the end of August at Altimonte Springs, in Orlando, Florida. Two weeks prior to the event, I joined the rest of Team GB at the Swiss Ski School in Clermont, about an hour's drive from Orlando, in order to train and acclimatise to American temperatures. Accommodation for our team of nine skiers, a manager, physiotherapist and a coach turned out to be one of several beautiful houses, each equipped with the latest mod cons, not to mention an outdoor swimming pool and a fantastic hot tub. Best of all, at the bottom of the garden, we had a private jetty jutting into the sparkling waters of Lake Denise. One of the team members walked with me around the house and gardens, describing the layout, allowing me to form a mental image that would, with the help of my cane, enable me to get about more independently.

Our team had the use of the lake every day from 7 a.m. until 2 p.m. when the Italian team took over. Initially, the early start caused a few sleepy groans but it wasn't long before we were thanking our lucky stars that we hadn't been allocated the afternoon session. With thunderstorms that arrived on schedule every day at 2.30 p.m., we were happy it was the Italian team and not us that endured a choppy ride. Naturally, when our rivals were within earshot, we made the appropriate noises of sympathy but, when the sky darkened and the thunder rolled, we couldn't help but voice our delight at being indoors.

As it was my first international trip with Team GB, I knew I'd be subject to some kind of initiation rite. I just didn't know when or what form it would take. When my coach advised me that it was about to rain and suggested I run upstairs and bring my washing in from the balcony, I didn't suspect a thing. Instead, I thanked him for his consideration and hurried off in search of my freshly laundered kit. Dressed in nothing but my bikini, I stepped onto the balcony only to be greeted by the laughter and cheers of my team-mates below, who then proceeded to turn the garden hose as well as a variety of water pistols on me, drenching me with a freezing spray. Later, as I walked back from the lake they tried to give me another soaking by giving me instructions to walk a little further to my right. But by then I had them sussed and, knowing they were guiding me towards the pool, retorted that I didn't fancy a swim just at the moment.

One of my team-mates, Sean, teased me mercilessly and refused to listen to my warning that, when least expected, I'd get my revenge. Eventually, when the guys were busy playing pool at the other end of the back porch, I grabbed the opportunity for a little pay back and crept into the kitchen and borrowed a cup of sugar. Quietly, I stole into Sean's bedroom and sprinkled a couple of handfuls between his bed sheets. I could barely suppress the giggles at the thought of

Sean and his sweet but very itchy dreams. As soon as I returned to the porch, I knew I'd been rumbled. The guys' joking and constant references to the word 'sugar' left me in no doubt they'd witnessed my dirty deed. Apparently, they'd seen me leave the kitchen and, knowing I was up to no good, gathered around the French windows of Sean's room to solve the mystery. I just had to laugh. In my determination to get a slice of revenge, I hadn't checked the position of the window in Sean's room. Still, I was glad to hear I'd passed the initiation rite with flying colours.

Morale continued to be upbeat as we enjoyed the great sense of bonding and camaraderie. But, unlike the weather, we couldn't predict the storm that waited to cast a cloud of gloom over the atmosphere. When Adelaine, one of the team's wheelchair users, injured her foot during training, no-one guessed the seriousness of her condition. However, an X-ray soon confirmed that her foot was broken and poor Adelaine wouldn't be able to compete. Affectionately known as Indie due to her tendency toward indecisiveness, Adelaine was one of our top skiers. Losing her was a real blow to the team and the collective mood took an immediate nosedive. But there was worse to come when we learned from Troy that Kevin, another of our squad members and Troy's best friend, had suffered a fatal asthma attack while attending a wedding in the UK. It was unbelievable. Just the week before, Kevin and I had stood on the dock at Heron Lake, sharing a joke and chatting. I recalled the profound nature of our conversation, never realising it would be our last. As we stood silently around the porch, stunned by shock, a common thread linked all our thoughts. The loss of our dear friend reminded each one of us that our hold on life is, at best, incredibly fragile. The burden of sadness weighed heavily and we knew that it would inevitably affect our performance in the competition. It was essential we regain some kind of equilibrium. In the end, we called a team meeting and, after a lot of discussion, unanimously decided that, in memory of Kevin, we would go out and give the performance of our careers. As it turned out, it was also the hardest fought competition of mine.

The Saturday before the event, we moved to the official hotel for the duration of the tournament. With a free day to relax, our team decided to go out and have some fun. As it was my birthday, I was given the choice of deciding where to spend the time. Orlando has a lot to offer but its theme parks are legendary. I opted to celebrate my big day at Islands of Adventure and the MGM studios. It was absolutely amazing. The park was huge, and moving from one attraction to another seemed more like a marathon than a simple stroll. We had to walk for miles but, as an elite athlete in peak physical condition, it didn't bother me. I really enjoyed the experience. I never could have imagined that the next time I visited I wouldn't be able to walk unaided.

Despite the interruption of sadness at the loss of Kevin, staying at the Swiss Ski School in Clermont had been a lot of fun. I loved the surroundings and enjoyed the company of the other team members who, as well as being great craic, were always considerate and helpful. Independence has always been important to me, and my friends ensured I had as much freedom as possible. But, almost as soon as I arrived at the official hotel at Crane's Roost, I realised things were going to be very different. I'd never stayed at the Embassy Suites Hotels before and the layout was both alien and unfamiliar, although I'm sure that with a little assistance from a particular member of the hotel staff, I could have learned to find my way around and make my stay more comfortable. Unfortunately, life is full of uncooperative people and I happened to meet one of them at Crane's Roost. It soon became apparent that the lady in question was not only unaware of my difficulties, but didn't want to know about them. Instead, she ignored my requests for help and left me to get on with it. I knew I had to report to reception the following morning but hadn't a clue how to get there. I asked the less than co-operative assistant, and her advice to take the lift, turn left, etc, may have been fine for an individual who can see where they are going but to a blind woman, it was incomprehensible. Still, I did try, although with little success. The arrival of any team is always a hectic time and marked by non-stop activity. A couple of our members had brought their young families along and, when not practising, were busy with them. Without Paul I felt lonely and isolated and was rapidly becoming more and more stressed. As usual, when feeling out of my depth, I turned to my husband, who was always able to pour a measure of comfort and restore calm. During our telephone conversation, the employee most in need of a customer service training programme burst into my room to announce that I was wanted in reception but would have to find my own way down. Despite overhearing the abrupt and aggressive tone, Paul said nothing. Not wanting my husband to worry or gauge my soaring levels of apprehension, I retorted that it was no problem, I'd be there shortly. Amazingly, I managed to do just that. However, Paul, who knows me so well, had picked up on my anxiety and, a short time later, rang back to say he had booked a flight and was on his way. I was ecstatic. With Paul at my side, I knew everything would be okay. I have to say that, apart from the receptionist from hell scenario, Crane's Roost enjoyed a fantastic location. The lake, directly across the road from our accommodation, was a beautiful place to spend a balmy evening. Coloured lights, a soft breeze and music wafting across the water make an excellent recipe for romance!

Music may be the food of love but, for me, it's pretty good for the nervous system when competing. Our team song was 'Hooked on a Feeling' by Blue and we requested that whenever one of us skied, it should be played over the sound system set up around the lake.

As I'd hoped, the prelims went well. I won the slalom prelim with a new European record and just a buoy short of the world record. I made a mental note that next time, I'd make sure to get out of the slalom gates a lot quicker. Tricks were also good. I didn't set any world records but I did win. The jump prelims were due to be held the following day and I couldn't help but wonder if Paul would arrive in time. To my delight he did, and with a new surge of confidence I set out to show him what I could do. There were a lot of cheers when I broke the world record but I think my husband was shouting and clapping loudest of all.

With the prelims out of the way, I turned my attention to the finals. Once again to the sound of music, I left the dock to compete in slalom. I'm still not certain what went wrong, but when I returned, I was not a happy bunny. I felt that my performance hadn't reached its usual high standard. The scores confirmed my worst nightmare. I had not emerged an outright winner as I'd intended. Instead, the Italian skier and I had tied first place. In order to determine the winner, there would have to be a ski-off where I would either come out on top or kiss the gold medal as well as my title goodbye. I'd witnessed this event on several occasions but always prayed it wouldn't happen to me. My feelings were in turmoil and I couldn't decide which was uppermost: I was horrified at being in such a predicament, fearful of the actual event and embarrassed at the prospect of letting the team down. Yet there was nothing else for it, I'd have to go through with it and give it my best shot.

My rival, Suzie from the Italian team, was first to compete. She chose a speed of 49 kph and, as she sped off, I waited with baited breath, listening intently for the bleeps from the audio slalom system. Suddenly, my ears pricked up. Suzie had missed buoy six and told me exactly what I needed to do. I decided to go out at a top speed of 55 kph. Concentrating, I focused on giving it my best effort. There was no room for error. I heard the bleep as I rounded buoy six and accelerated out the slalom gates, body tense as I waited for the double bleep to indicate a clear pass. A fraction of a second later, I had what I wanted. I'd done it. I had won with a new world record. My dream as well as my title was still firmly intact. To the sound of my team's cheers, I skied back towards the dock, laughing with relief as well as the exhilaration of winning. Paul was waiting to add his congratulations and I knew he was incredibly proud of me.

Once slalom was over, I turned my attention to tricks. Any residual nerves had been washed away in the ski-off so I was fairly calm for my least favourite discipline and felt I'd performed quite well. To my annoyance, the scoreboard revealed that the judges didn't share my opinion and had neglected to mark two of my tricks. With so much at stake, there was nothing else for it but to ask my team captain to lodge a formal complaint. This procedure involves a strict code of practice that requires five World Class J1 judges to re-play and scrutinise videos of the event before making a final judgement. Waiting for the result was a nerve-racking experience, as I knew that the outcome could mean the difference between winning gold or winning gold with a world record. The former may be a great personal achievement but the latter would provide some much-needed team points. Two hours later, the verdict arrived along with an apology. I had indeed been marked incorrectly when two of my tricks had been overlooked. I was overjoyed and greatly relieved when the scores were amended and I was awarded the world record as well as the extra team points.

The following day, I stood on the dock in the hot August sunshine and prepared to compete in the final discipline of the tournament. As usual, music lent a bit of inspiration, and for this event I always chose the very appropriate and classic rendition of Van Halen's 'Jump'.

The slight breeze helped buoy my confidence of a good score as a little head wind helps blow away the backwash from the previous skier, making jumping conditions perfect. As my guide Gordon and I prepared to ski, I knew the crowd was watching and that Paul wasn't among the onlookers. He hates to see me jump and usually goes for a walk whenever I'm about to perform. Although on this occasion, if he had known I was going to throw in an unusual trick, he might have stayed around! Just as we prepared to leave the dock, I noticed that weather conditions had changed and the earlier breeze had disappeared. Gordon didn't seem too concerned and assured me I'd be fine but as we entered the jump course and he shouted the countdown, I felt my skis begin to bounce violently. Suddenly, before I realised what was happening, I landed on the ramp, my skis slipped from beneath me and I was left hanging upside down in the air. To add to my indignity, a helicopter flew overhead with a television crew on board making sure they missed none of the action. An incorrect landing may be embarrassing but it can also be extremely painful. By the time I was facing right way up and had regained my composure, my left leg was throbbing. But with only two jumps left in a world championship competition, I had no time to worry about physical injuries. I had to ignore the pain and get on with it. Shaking with nerves, I went around for jump number two. Gordon, sensing my fear, reassured me that the approach to the ramp was looking good and, to my relief, he was right this time. I landed safely on the other side, facing in the right direction. The third jump was just as successful but by the time I'd reached the dock, adrenaline levels had subsided and the pain from my leg was really beginning to intensify. Nevertheless, I was ecstatic and looked forward to, once again, taking my place on the winner's podium.

That evening the awards ceremony was an unusually emotional experience for me. I had won four gold medals for audio slalom, tricks and jump and taken the overall title. I'd also broken the world record in each of the three disciplines and earned maximum team points. The only note of disappointment was that a small difference of 200 points meant that our team had taken silver instead of gold. America had beaten us on their home waters. Yet, it was a good incentive for us to do better. While I was deeply honoured to achieve so much for my country, there was a personal aspect to the 2003 competition that touched me deeply. I simply hadn't been prepared for the overt display of respect and affection shown by my peers. Shaking my hand, they congratulated and commended me on a hard-won victory and made my success taste even sweeter.

With the ceremony over, it was time to party! Around midnight, we walked along the deserted shores of the lake towards the little town of Altimonte Springs, where we knew we'd find a bar. On route, a jeep pulled alongside and the Australian coach, Ryan Green, asked if any of us wanted a lift. A few of us decided to accept his invitation and immediately climbed on board. I sat in the back seat while Paul rode tailgate and several of our wheelchair-user friends held on to his outstretched legs and were towed slowly along behind. Occasionally, when we hit a bump in the road, we'd lose one of our wheelies and it was my job to shout 'skier down, have to do a re-run!' Our unusual convoy must have made a comical sight but when a couple of policemen pulled us over, we thought the fun was finally over. However, they seemed to share our sense of humour and instead of giving us a stern lecture, provided us with an escort into town. It was hilarious and the party turned out to be the best ever. We made a lot of new friends but the 2003 competitions taught me a lot about myself as an athlete. I discovered through the slalom ski-off that I could find inner reserves of strength and determination when necessary. In tricks, I'd been able to keep a cool head and let my performance speak for itself. I'd confronted every skier's worst nightmare in the jump discipline and not only survived but won. I left the tournament with more than I anticipated. I had a new appreciation of my ability to succeed. I had no idea it was about to be put to the ultimate test.

The season ended on yet another positive note when, for the third time, I won the Belfast Telegraph's Sports Personality of the Year award. Boy, was I riding on the crest of a wave!

Chapter 13
The Accident

There's an old adage that says the book of life has two sides to every page. We fill one with our plans and dreams while providence writes on the other. Yet, what it ordains seldom coincides with our goals. When I arrived at McCormick Ski School in February 2004, my main objective was to improve my overall technique. It seems that providence had an entirely different and more sinister agenda. I had no idea that, by the end of March, instead of battling for medals, I'd be fighting for my life.

For the first month, things couldn't have gone better. Still on a high from my success at the 2003 Worlds, morale was up. The intensive training schedule was hard work but the Florida sunshine felt good on my face and as I skied around the lake, it felt great to be alive. Even my performance appeared to be going from strength to strength. It seemed that the more I skied, the better it flowed. Slalom in particular was progressing extremely well and I was jubilant that I'd finally cracked it.

Tricks, always my least favourite, had improved enormously. Without a horizon to provide focus, it's difficult for blind skiers to make a lot of headway in this discipline.

Apart from the lack of visual aid, it isn't always easy to feel the top of the wake in order to rotate. At times I hated tricks and moaned about doing them but when it came to the overall title, they were essential. Yet, as my coach pointed out, they were becoming much better and the recent standard was also proving a lot more consistent.

Contrary to my lack of enthusiasm for tricks, I simply loved to jump. Throughout the training sessions, I was achieving good distances and was thrilled when my coach suggested I buy longer skis that would help increase my distance even further. Elated, I rang Connelly Skis and immediately ordered a pair of 84 inch jump skis. Those few weeks at ski school were amazing. It seemed I was riding high and nothing could go wrong.

Before beginning another three weeks of training, I flew home for a fortnight's rest and to see Paul. I made a habit of calling Paul a couple of times a day while I was away but there was no substitute for actually being with him. We talked excitedly about the forthcoming Florida Open Competitions, an able-bodied event, and were both quietly confident I'd do well. The days flew by and before we realised, it was time for me to travel back to Tampa. Paul's suggestion that he join me for the week leading up to the Open Competitions, when we could spend the time exploring the Florida Keys, sounded like a real adventure. As I boarded the plane, my head was swimming with all the lovely things life had in store.

Back at ski school, I couldn't wait to try out my new jump skis. Naturally, as I needed to get a feel for the skis and test them out on the water, it would take a while before I'd actually go over the ramp. Still, once I felt comfortable, it would be a real treat to find out how much my distance would improve. There was a lot of work to be done out on the lake but first I had a score to settle on dry land.

Everyone in the team knew how much I loved the subtropical temperatures but it was also common knowledge that, although I didn't appreciate the thought of alligators nibbling my toes, I'm absolutely petrified of snakes. The lads couldn't resist teasing me and took every opportunity to throw a rubber hose in my direction, making me believe it was a python or one of its many cousins. Many times, I tried to use logic and tell myself, 'if you can't see it Janet, it isn't there.' Somehow, I never quite believed my own counsel. Judging by the number of pranks, my hysterical screams must have provided the boys with an endless source of amusement.

However, on one occasion, the joke went a little too far when Ben, another skier, came running towards me shouting that he'd found his first snake. Despite my warning him not to bring the creature anywhere near me, he insisted on cornering me on the dock. Hemmed between the reptile and the lake I turned to dive into the water and swim to safety but my coach grabbed my arm and assured me it was only the old rubber hose trick again. While Ben held the so-called reptile, my coach kept hold of my arm and insisted I reach out and touch it. I have to admit, I was terrified but even more scared of appearing foolish, so I stretched out my hand and did as he said. To my horror, my fingers touched a smooth, silky, and very much alive creature. It was indeed a snake. Mingled with the echo of my screams, the last thing I heard was the hysterical laughter of Ben and the coach.

Like all athletes, I sustain my fair share of minor injuries and tend to use Ralgex, a common preparation that sends an intense heat into the aching muscle. After the episode with the snake, I decided to get my own back by adding a little heat to Ben's nether regions. As soon as he had left for the lake I, with the help of an accomplice, nipped into the changing rooms and sprayed his shorts with a layer of inner warmth. Then my co-conspirator and I relaxed in the hot tub and waited for the entertainment to begin. It didn't take long for the treatment to work its magic. The sound of Ben's angry expletives told us it wasn't only his temper that was red hot. When he demanded to know who had been at his shorts with a burst of Ralgex, I merely smiled and said, 'Ralgex, what on earth is that?' My revenge tasted very sweet.

On Thursday 25 March, I was delighted to find my new skis had arrived. The following Monday morning, my coach had set them up for me and I looked forward to trying them out in the afternoon. With lunch over, all the students lined their jump skis up on the dock and started to prepare for training. It was a beautiful day. The sun was shining, temperatures hovered around ninety-five degrees and with just a little head wind, conditions for skiing were perfect. My new, longer skis were in the line-up and I couldn't wait to try them out. My coach assured me that their additional length would, if anything, make them more stable than my old ones and probably feel a bit more comfortable. As I was finishing off a few warm-up exercises, the phone rang and I was delighted to hear Paul's voice. We chatted for a few minutes about the new skis, laughed at my prank on Ben and generally indulged in a bit of homely gossip. I knew the coach frowned upon personal calls interrupting training but I couldn't resist a long-distance natter. At the sound of the coach's exasperated tone, I knew it was time to end the conversation and with a quick 'I love you' and a promise to call him later, I hung up. Those were the last words I would say to Paul for a very long time.

With my stretching routine complete, I picked up my ski handle, gloves and cane and made my way down the jetty. Carefully, I stepped over the other students' skis until I came to mine which, in order to save confusion, I always mark with Braille. As usual, I went through the procedure of dipping each ski in the water, applying some washing-up liquid and slipping my feet easily inside. It was a hot afternoon and, as I wasn't going over the ramp, I'd abandoned the heavy jump suit and helmet in favour of a lightweight pair of shorts, a ski-top and my life jacket. I was merely going to tour the lake, enjoy the feel of the sun and spray of the water on my face and have some fun. That was my intention. I didn't yet know what providence had entered in my particular book of life.

Ready and waiting on the dock, I heard the boat arrive with the previous student. Normally, when it's my turn to train, my coach Michael runs down the dock and jumps on board. On this occasion, fate decreed otherwise and at the realisation Michael wasn't coming, I threw my ski handle to the coach already in the boat and shouted instructions to the driver as to speed, boat path and signals. Seated on the edge of the dock with the sun beating down on me, I waited to go and reflected on how lucky I was. Yes, life had dealt me a tragic blow when I'd lost my sight. At the time it had seemed like the end of the world and that I'd never find happiness again. Now, with a happy marriage, a sport I was passionate about and the honour of skiing for my country, I felt like the luckiest woman alive!

At the feel of the boat taking up slack, I shouted 'hit it' and prepared to go. The instruction to 'hit it' is a standard command and is deliberately chosen to avoid any confusion between 'go' or 'no'. Those two little words are clear and concise, leaving no margin for error. I felt the rope tighten and, leaving the dock behind, I waited for the whistle signal to tell me to begin skiing. But suddenly, without warning, there was what I can only describe as a massive impact. For a fraction of a second my brain tried to compute what had happened but gave up the struggle and mercifully succumbed to the comfort of unconsciousness. As I would later learn, I had been skied at high speed into the huge metal ramp situated in the middle of the lake.

The next thing I recall was the mingled sounds of water lapping round me, the boat's engine and voices shrill with panic shouting instructions. With my upper body held above the water and drifting in and out of consciousness, I was towed behind the boat and back to the dock. In the following weeks, I would often think how I might have made a tasty meal for any passing predator. Back at the dock, I soon discovered that it was Tanya, the boat driver, who had held me for the worst journey of my life. Her slightest movement was enough to send an excruciating pain up my leg and through my entire body. I tried to feel the extent of my injuries by moving my right hand over my pelvis but the shock of bone sticking through my shorts was almost heart stopping. Once more, I attempted to gauge the damage, this time using my left hand. But it refused to co-operate and lay limply at my side. The sound of a helicopter told me the paramedics had arrived, but as they climbed into the water in order to examine me before moving me onto a stretcher, the agony was unbearable and sent me spiralling back into a cocoon of oblivion. Apart from my face, blood was pouring from a huge open wound at the top of my leg and the medical team needed to remove my shorts. As I drifted upward towards reality, I realised what they were about to do and desperately tried to tell them not to ruin my shorts. Under the circumstances, it may sound a strange request but, as I've since learned, it was a perfectly natural response. Apparently, when confronted by major trauma, the brain, unable to absorb the shock, closes down and focuses on something trivial and less demanding. For me, my shattered bones were secondary. The only thing that seemed to matter was the preservation of my little neoprene ski shorts. Yet despite my best efforts, I couldn't get the words past my mouth. Something was horribly wrong with my face. The sickly, coppery taste of blood was filling my mouth, running down my throat, choking me, making it impossible to get air into my lungs. I was suffocating.

The last thing I recall was an injection of pain relief and a helicopter ride to the trauma unit at Tampa General Hospital. I owe a great debt of gratitude to the pilot and helicopter crew whose expertise and professionalism got me to hospital in the fastest time possible.

Apart from my coach Michael and his friend Tanya, who called a few times to ask about my condition, no-one from the ski school visited. Alone and unconscious, with no provision of records or personal details, I was known to staff in the intensive care unit as Jane Doe. At the time the apparent lack of interest went unnoticed. After all, drifting through oblivion, I'd no idea who was or wasn't present. Although I have to confess that, on reflection, I found the scenario upsetting and disappointing. Doctors assessing the extent of my injuries were united in their prognosis: I wouldn't survive the night. Yet they continued to help me fight. The massive trauma to my face prevented me from breathing and an emergency tracheotomy had to be performed. I had been whipped into the ramp at the velocity required to rip a seat belt in two with the result that the bones in my face, including eye sockets, cheek bones, and nose were completely smashed. My jaw was dislocated and suffered multiple fractures plus I lost several teeth. My right hip and pelvis were dislocated and broken as was my left elbow. The head of my femur was crushed, my knee-cap fractured, ribs were also dislocated. I suffered crush injuries, snapped a tendon in my thumb and lost a serious amount of blood. My face was gone, my body a mangled mess and my heart failed on three occasions. But doctors resuscitated me, allowing me to cling tentatively to life. I will never know whether it was a dream or a moment of lucidity but I remember thinking, I am going to die here alone and I didn't get to say goodbye to Paul and my family.

Back in Belfast, Paul was waiting for my call. My accident happened at 2 p.m. Florida time, but at 7 p.m. in Belfast my husband was waiting to hear how I'd enjoyed the new skis. When the phone rang, he expected to hear the usual 'Hi honey' followed by a detailed account of my day. As he picked up the phone, the smile died on his lips when instead of my excited prattle, he heard the gravity in my coach's voice as he explained that I'd been involved in a serious accident and that Paul had better book a flight immediately. Stunned, he rang the hospital where doctors explained the critical nature of my condition. The only advice they could offer was that Paul should contact a funeral director before leaving the country as I wouldn't be coming home alive.

Disorientated and shocked, Paul rang his mum and my parents asking them to come to our house immediately. My poor mum, as soon as she heard about the accident, could think of nothing but getting Paul off the phone as quickly as possible. Like all mothers, her first instinct was to hear the voice of her child. Nothing else would offer the reassurance she so badly needed. Life hadn't been easy for Mum. She had been forced to watch helplessly as glaucoma stole first her husband's sight, then her children's. But when asked how she'd coped, she simply replied that it was a case of putting one foot in front of the other and getting through life one day at a time. Although my parents were pleased that water-skiing had provided me with an enjoyable new career, both worried constantly about the dangers of the sport. When they learned that I had attempted and then mastered jumping, it added a new dimension to their parental concern. In fact, I think Pop thought I must have gone a little crazy! Mum said little, but it took a long time before she could summon up the courage to watch me jump. I think parenthood must be an extremely difficult role, especially when children become adults and immune to advice.

Mum's insistence that she call the hospital and speak to me provided Paul with a bit of a dilemma. There was no way he could tell her I was in a coma, never mind the awful prognosis. Sensing her panic, he ignored his own distress and calmly asked to speak with Pop who, once he'd learned I'd been airlifted to hospital, grasped the urgency of the situation. I don't know how they managed it but somehow, by the end of the call, Mum had been soothed and persuaded that it was essential she take over the business and allow Paul to leave immediately for Florida. We were going to need every penny we could get.

Functioning on autopilot, Paul found himself at the door of our next door neighbours, Lyn and Warren, who, seeing his distress, took control of the situation and packed his suitcase. Other friends began searching the internet for the next available flight. Everything was arranged and then Paul suddenly discovered he didn't have a passport. We'd been due to go on holiday in the Florida Keys and Paul had applied for his passport to be renewed, but unfortunately it hadn't arrived. Normally the delay wouldn't have mattered but no-one could have predicted such tragic circumstances.

In the end Jeffrey Donaldson, our local politician, came to the rescue. The MP kindly arranged for the passport office to open at 6 a.m., allowing Paul to pick up his necessary documentation on the way to the airport. In order to make sure he didn't miss it, the plane had to be delayed. It seems that the Gray family play havoc with the airlines' flight schedules. I can't imagine the stress Paul must have been under as he made the four-thousand-mile trip across the Atlantic, unsure of what he'd find on the other side. Later, he would paint me a vivid picture of the gut-wrenching journey where, despite speeds of over 500 mph, time appeared to stand still. Instinctively, he needed to do something to help but trapped in the body of a jumbo jet thousands of miles above the ground, he could do nothing but allow memories to wash over him and wait. We'd been through so much together. He had been my rock, never allowing blindness to exempt me from the experiences of life. When others tried to imprison me behind bars of well-meaning concern, Paul set me free and encouraged me to get out there and have a go. On that long, lonely flight, his mind turned over my devastating list of injuries. He wasn't a doctor but it didn't take a medical degree to figure out I was a mess. Yet, he did not believe for an instant that I would die. His confidence was not founded in logic. Instead Paul relied on the intangible yet timeless evidence of instinct. Outwardly, circumstances may have pointed to a tragic end to our story, but an inner voice convinced him there were still many more chapters to be written.

Chapter 14
Oblivion

It had taken glaucoma years to steal my sight completely. As my vision deteriorated I had teetered on the brink of the sighted world, fighting the condition's relentless assault. Eventually, when surgeons lost the battle to save my remaining vision, I was immediately toppled into darkness. But, I had survived. Despite chains of fear and insecurity, I had clambered out of my prison and built a new life. Yet, just when I'd reached the summit of success, fate once again intervened. In a split second, I was changed from an elite athlete in peak physical condition to a helpless woman trapped inside a broken and useless body.

Before leaving Belfast, Paul had promised my mum to bring me home alive. However, when he arrived at Tampa General Hospital, he still had no idea what to expect. He had been prepared for the worst possible scenario but when he was ushered into the intensive care unit and saw the body prostrate on the bed, machines sustaining her life, he instinctively breathed a sigh of relief. There was no way this woman was his wife. Doctors must have made some ghastly mistake. The Janet he knew and loved was tall and slim with blonde hair and blue eyes that, he often joked, twinkled with mischief. This lady was a stranger. Her hair, matted with blood, had no definable colour as it clung in lifeless strands to her head. Instead of agile limbs that could manoeuvre skis effortlessly through a slalom course, perform tricks or sail over a jump ramp, the swollen body seemed ungainly and bloated. Searching the featureless and broken face, he could find no trace of the woman he loved. However, Paul's relief was short-lived. My body may have seemed alien and unfamiliar yet it is impossible to share someone's life without absorbing some essence of their innermost being. Paul may not have recognised my form or face but he knew without doubt I was the woman he had married and his denial gradually gave way to the emotional trauma of reality. Gently he took my hand and told me that he was with me and that everything would be alright. Lost in oblivion, I didn't hear those first words of reassurance but later in my brief interludes of consciousness, he would repeat them again and again, giving me the immeasurable comfort of a love that, since we met, has been unconditional.

Doctors, used to dealing with the shocked relatives of massive trauma victims, are experts at leading the way towards acceptance. Understanding that families find it difficult to absorb the totality of the situation, medical staff feed information in tolerable bites. While Paul couldn't digest the full range of my injuries, he was able to comprehend the overall seriousness of my condition. Dr Halpern gently explained that I was in a coma and was depending on a mechanical ventilator to keep me alive. The chances of my survival were negligible. Yet, despite the gravity of the prognosis, Paul stalwartly refused to believe that I would die. Instead, he began to focus on the long, slow haul towards my eventual recovery. Like me, my husband is a fighter.

After carrying out an emergency tracheotomy, infusing me with endless units of blood, and dealing with three successive heart attacks, the doctors decided to set about repairing my broken body. First on the list was my shattered elbow. As the accident had occurred on the lake, the open wound at the top of my leg had become badly infected and would have to wait until antibiotics took effect and controlled the infection. Meantime, a drain was put in place with a view to operating at a later date. My next recollection was the arrival of the orthopaedic surgeon to remove the tube. His warning that it was going to be painful was, to say the least, an under-statement. Despite a few additional and desperate pushes on my morphine pump, the agony still managed to send me hurtling back into unconsciousness.

Once surgeons had put my femur, hip and pelvis back together, it was time to rebuild my face.

Dr Halpern, realising the traumatic nature of this surgery, kindly took Paul for a coffee and gently explained what he intended to do. Once he'd outlined the lengthy and intricate procedure of re-constructing my jaw, nose, cheekbones and eye sockets, he asked Paul if he had a photograph of me that he could use as a guide. The only picture Paul had was the one from my passport and it is a real testimony to the expertise and skill of this professional man that he was able to do so much with such basic material. Beginning with my jaw, Doctor Halpern slowly and painstakingly put my face back together. However, with so little to go on, he had to rely on the old-fashioned method of wiring my jaw through the gum and around every tooth. The operation took eight hours and, as it sounds, was incredibly painful for months afterwards!

While I spent most of the first week either in the operating theatre or a drugged haze, poor Paul, dressed in a shirt and tie, wandered the streets of Tampa trying to fill time. His dress code wasn't exactly suited to the subtropical climate but, understandably, when he left Belfast, clothing was the last thing on his mind. Nevertheless, in temperatures of over ninety degrees Fahrenheit he must have felt a bit on the hot side! Initially, he booked into a local hotel but when doctors advised him that I would need to be hospitalised for at least four months, Paul realised that such an extended stay would have huge implications on his business and our financial situation, which, given the circumstances, we could ill afford. In an attempt to find a more practical solution, he began making enquiries about renting one of the nearby houses that were owned by the hospital. As the condition of trauma victims can deteriorate rapidly, the purpose-built accommodation enabled families to be with their loved ones at a moment's notice, any time of the night or day. Paul then contacted my family, who agreed it would be best if they all took turns to be with me. While Paul returned to oversee his business, my parents or Ian would fly out and take his place.

Paul's constant contact with home kept everyone informed of the situation and although Mum's instinct had been to fly out to Florida along with Paul, she was in no state to make the journey. When it came to water-skiing, I may have been the champion of the world but to Mum, I was just Janet, her little girl. The emotional toll on my parents was indescribable. As soon as my brother Ian heard the news, he knew my parents would be distraught and immediately packed a bag and moved into the family home. We are a close family and it's in times of crisis that I really appreciate the strong nature of our bond.

Gradually, I was able to breathe on my own and didn't need the ventilator. During the second week, sedatives were slowly reduced and I was conscious a little more often but totally unable to move or speak. No doubt a lot of men would think a silent partner sheer bliss. But for Paul, the sound of my voice was the only thing he wanted to hear, while his quiet reassuring tones helped calm and soothe me. Having him around made me feel safe and protected.

As the days passed, my inability to communicate became more frustrating. I wanted to ask questions, talk to Paul and generally feel a bit more in control. Fortunately, we managed to come up with a solution. As my right hand was still in one piece, nurses rigged up a clipboard and I was able to scribble messages, although I had to be quick as I never knew when I would suddenly nod off again. Very often Paul was left with a totally incomprehensible scrawl because I'd fallen asleep mid-sentence. When I next woke I couldn't remember what I'd intended to say. Paul has since told me that, sometimes when he arrived at the unit, he'd find a note waiting for him, asking, 'Where's my coffee?!' It seems that no matter how ill or the fact that I couldn't eat or drink, my sense of humour had survived intact.

Despite the moments of wakefulness, my time in Tampa General Hospital was characterised by agonising pain. Days and nights merged in a kaleidoscope of snatched conversations, medical procedures and the intense lights of an operating theatre. Initially, as my face was swollen to three times its normal size, my eyelids had to be stitched closed. But I can still recall the terror of having my eye sockets reconstructed. Anxious, scared, and finding it difficult to breathe, I was wheeled into theatre where the intense heat from the overhead lights increased my panic, making me feel extremely nauseous. The tube in my throat added to my dread of being sick as, lying flat on my back, with no way to lift my head or turn, I was petrified of choking to death. The sense of fear over-rode any desire to hit the morphine button and relieve the pain. Helpless, there was nothing I could do but lie still, endure the agony and wait for it to be over. Later, in the recovery room, the sickness continued to wash over me in unrelenting waves and to my horror, I ended up spraying everything in the vicinity with a vibrant shade of red. Thankfully, nurses are used to the sight of blood and they dealt with the situation calmly and efficiently. One young woman in particular realised my fears and would often scold me for not making more use of the pain relief. In fact, very often at the sight of me flinching, she would take control of the situation, hit the morphine button a few hard thumps and deliver me a hefty dose.

As far as Paul was concerned, I was the most important patient in Tampa General. However, as shock subsided and time moved on, he began to notice the familiar lines of worry and fear etched on the faces of those around him and realised that other people were also suffering. One Mexican family in particular caught his attention and before long, they were sharing the miserable story of lives interrupted by tragedy. Apparently, the little group had arrived to spend a fun-packed vacation in Florida. Filled with excitement and overwhelmed by the sights, the young father had tried to capture the atmosphere on camera. Unfortunately, just as he stepped off the pavement to find the angle, he was struck by a passing bus. Instead of Disneyland, the poor holiday-makers spent their time in the trauma unit of a hospital waiting to see if their loved one survived. Although we would have liked to have known the outcome of their story, the opportunity never arose. Hopefully, like me, the young man clung to life and was finally restored to his family.

While Paul kept my family informed, a journalist from the local newspaper, *The Tampa Tribune*, published an article and told the rest of the world. I'd done a few interviews with the paper and when they heard there had been a horrific skiing accident, they lost no time in finding the details. Once published, it didn't take long for editors in New York to latch on to the information that an Irish skier was fighting for her life in Florida. Within a few days, Irish journalists were running the story as headline news. The reaction was immediate and overwhelming. Everyone wanted to hear about my progress and, while Mum and Pop did their best to reassure relatives abroad, Paul tried to keep local media at home updated. As word of the accident spread, churches around the world prayed and said masses for my survival.

Back in Ulster, school children sent text messages to their friends, asking them to 'pray for Janet'. I may have been oblivious to all the spiritual input on my behalf but I am eternally grateful. There is no doubt I knocked on those pearly gates several times but thanks to the intervention of thousands I will never meet, the heavenly hosts refused to let me in. My survival is a testimony to the power of prayer, and perhaps my life has some unfulfilled purpose I've yet to accomplish. Apart from divine petitions, I was blessed with a visit from a Christian lady who worshipped at the local Free Presbyterian Church and, after learning from a friend at home that I was at death's door, decided to post a watch at my bedside so that I would not die alone. I am so grateful for the many lonely hours she passed while waiting for Paul's arrival.

Before any skiing event, Paul and I always ensure we invest in adequate insurance cover. However, no-one could have anticipated the seriousness of the accident or how costly my hospitalisation would prove. While my life hung in the balance, hospital administrators and insurance representatives wrangled and argued over money. Paul, in a constant round of telephone calls and insurance reports, tried desperately to ensure I had the necessary care. It must have been extremely difficult for him to haggle over finance when caught in the deepest throes of stress. Nevertheless, an airlift to hospital, emergency procedures, endless surgery, reconstruction of my face, not to mention four months of hospitalisation and God knows how many more of physiotherapy and rehabilitation, meant insurance bosses were running scared. The longer I stayed in America, the more it was going to cost them. The best scenario to help curtail any further outlay was to get me home, where the National Health Service could take over and pay for my treatment. Despite his desire to get me back to familiar surroundings, Paul knew I was in no fit state to travel and argued constantly with insurance administrators. Dr Halpern also expressed his objections but at the end of the day, finance dictated the outcome and it was decreed that, after my final life-saving operation, I would be flown by air ambulance to Northern Ireland and then taken to the trauma unit of Belfast's Royal Victoria Hospital. Unaware of this turn of events, my parents had already booked their flight to Florida and, with no hope of redress, lost the full fare of over £900.

In complete contrast to the insurance company's harshness, the staff at Tampa General couldn't have been kinder. As consciousness returned for longer periods, my awareness of pain increased. Most nights, the agonising bolts that shot through my body chased away any hope of sleep. At these times I turned to my talking books to provide distraction and help me make it through the night. One of the male nurses happened to notice my little talking machine and showed great kindness and consideration by bringing me lots of discs to keep me entertained. While impossible to single out any individual for the extreme level of care I was shown, I did grow increasingly fond of a young nurse who never failed to bring a note of happiness when she was around. Every morning, I would listen for her voice as she called a cheery greeting and stopped for a chat as soon as she came on duty. I remember how, over the days, the condition of my hair had become more and more annoying. Apart from the ability to move and breathe without restriction, I missed feeling clean and fresh. Compared to the life-threatening nature of my injuries, not to mention my poor featureless face, a lack of personal grooming may seem the least of my worries. But I'm sure that any woman who hasn't washed her hair in a couple of weeks, never mind having it plastered to her skull and caked with dried blood, will understand the desire for a bit of sprucing up. I knew that a wash and blow dry would be out of the question but I decided to ask if there was anything the medical profession could do to make me feel a little more feminine. My lovely nurse read my note and agreed I could do with some cosmetic intervention. Using a specially heated cap impregnated with shampoo, she gently removed the worst of the debris and left me feeling a lot more presentable. My face may have been swollen beyond recognition and my jaw clamped shut with wires but at least my hair was almost clean again!

As preparations for my departure got under way, doctors gave Paul a long list of medications essential to the trip and sent him off to the nearest pharmacy. The drug store turned out to have something in common with the local hamburger joint. They may dispense vastly different products but both operated a 'drive through' system. With no car, my poor husband had no choice but to take his place in the long line of cars and wait his turn. The look on the guy's face when Paul appeared at the window must have been a real scream. He didn't know what to make of the guy who arrived at the drive-in minus a car. Maybe when he heard his Irish accent, he drew his own conclusions.

If the young pharmacist thought Paul a trifle eccentric, the hospital staff believed he was crazy. Only a madman would walk through the streets of Tampa carrying a bag filled to the brim with expensive drugs. I couldn't help but laugh when, in the coming weeks, Paul told me about his American adventure. Apparently, on his return to the hospital, he'd met a man fishing from the bridge and, as he waited for the signal to cross, sat down to keep him company. Little did the local know that the stranger, who was listening so intently to his fishy tales, had a bag filled with hypodermic syringes and ampoules of morphine.

Naturally, I didn't fully appreciate the implications of a long-haul flight. All I knew was that I was finally going home. As much as I appreciated the expertise and kindness of the staff at Tampa General Hospital, I longed for the familiarity of an Ulster accent. I wanted to hear Mum's voice, to feel the gentle pressure of Pop's hand and to know that my brother Ian was encouraging and supporting us all. Ian and I are extremely close and have shared many of life's ups and downs. As well as understanding and empathising with me, he makes me laugh and, regardless of circumstances, leaves me feeling on top of the world. These were the people I needed around me. As my favourite nurse fussed over my hair, preparing me for the journey ahead, I felt the first stirrings of hope. After all, I had beaten the odds. I should have been dead, yet here I was, going home to the family and friends I thought I'd never meet again. Determination flickered, then roared into life. I was a fighter. It would be a long hard slog, but I would overcome because I was born to be a winner.

Chapter 15
Home Again

Two weeks after my near-fatal collision with a ski ramp, I was discharged from Tampa General Hospital, loaded into an ambulance and sent on my way to Orlando International Airport where a flight waited to take me to London. It wasn't the first time I'd made the 4,000 mile trip to Gatwick but on this occasion the experience seemed strangely surreal. Instead of skis and suitcases, I had tubes, drips and a heart monitor. But it wasn't only my luggage that was different. I'd never crossed the Atlantic dressed in a huge nightshirt emblazoned with pink flamingos and a pair of matching bed-socks. When Paul went shopping for something for me to wear, fashion or style didn't enter the equation. The only criterion was to find something roomy enough to cover my badly swollen body, as my ordinary clothes no longer fitted.

Up until the moment we left Tampa General Hospital, Paul continued to express his concern at the wisdom of the decision. It didn't take a degree in medicine to comprehend the severe nature of the risks involved. Just a few days previously, I was depending on a machine to keep me alive. I had endured endless hours of gruelling surgery, my leg was badly swollen and the wound was covered with a special heavy dressing. My face was totally unrecognisable and without a tube in my throat, breathing was an impossibility. For any patient with such extensive and serious injuries, leaving the intensive care unit was inconceivable. But to board a long-haul flight where thrombosis was a real concern for healthy individuals seemed an act of madness. Yet, we had no choice. When Paul arrived for his usual morning visit and found my bed empty, he immediately panicked. A recently vacated and neatly made bed on any ICU ward is not a good indication that the patient is doing well. Panicked and fearful, he immediately set off in search of an explanation and although relieved that I hadn't deteriorated further, was aghast that I was being prepared for an immediate departure. Sedatives may have been reduced to allow me brief periods of consciousness but the heavy doses of pain relief not only took the edge off the agony but managed to dull the frightening reality of my situation. The full implications of going home may not have penetrated my understanding but I knew from Paul's worried tone that I might be in for more than I bargained for.

Before leaving hospital, Paul and I were introduced to the specialist nurses who had arrived from Canada to accompany us on the journey. As well as carrying an array of drugs and needles, both wore a little backpack that was linked to me by a series of wires, enabling them to monitor my vital signs. The first hurdle was to lift me from the hospital bed and onto a stretcher, but before attempting the procedure the chief nurse asked me to indicate my level of pain by using a score of one to ten. I held up four fingers and gave him the thumbs up, meaning it was tolerable and I didn't want morphine. The last thing I needed on the long trip was the awful sensation of nausea that sometimes accompanied the drug. Thankfully, he didn't listen to me. Realising how agonising the movement would be, he gave me the maximum dose of pain relief and spared me the worst of the torture.

The journey to the airport took over three hours but at one stage, when our driver braked suddenly and without warning, it looked as though we might end up back at Tampa General. Uptight and stressed, Paul found it impossible to keep his cool and gave the man a piece of his mind. Fortunately, I was still heavily sedated and didn't fully appreciate how close I'd come to yet another accident.

Almost as soon as we arrived at Orlando International Airport, I began to wonder if our driver had taken a wrong turn and entered some crazy parallel universe. I couldn't believe my ears when airport officials insisted I be wheeled up to the reception desk to join the queue and check in as normal. Surely they could tell that my swollen, featureless face bore no resemblance to the picture in my passport. I lay there in my large printed nightshirt with nothing but a flimsy blanket to cover me, feeling very exposed and vulnerable. I think, for the first time since losing my sight, I was actually glad to be blind. At least I couldn't see the curious, pitiful stares of other passengers. Poor Paul was furious and left the staff in no doubt as to his feelings. The nurses, both experienced, professional air ambulance personnel, were equally appalled at such a display of gross insensitivity. With the check-in complete, we made our way to the security zone but any relief that my ordeal was over was short-lived. In fact, things were about to get even more weird. To our amazement, the guard on duty decided my trolley was a threat to public safety and asked me to hop off and allow him to carry out a search. My first thought was that the man was either blind or incredibly stupid but with no way to communicate, I had to leave Paul and the nurses to convince him that if he didn't let me through, he too might be in need of a hospital trolley. The fury in Paul's voice was unmistakable. I don't think I've ever heard him so angry although, on reflection, the time that I ignored his advice and added jump to my disciplines came pretty close. In the end, the security official allowed me and my trolley to pass but not before a muttered complaint that my face didn't look anything like the image in my passport.

The serious nature of my injuries meant that the nurses would have to carry out various medical procedures throughout the trip. In order to provide a quiet and clean environment, we had arranged for a room to be made available in the British Airways departure lounge, but to my horror, the official on duty took one look at my face, asked whether I was contagious and refused to let me in. It occurred to me that I may be in a critical condition but these guys were definitely unstable. By this stage, Paul's blood pressure as well as his temper was rocketing to dangerous levels. The nurses were speechless at the unbelievable level of incompetence but the necessity of adhering to a strict medical regime to keep my lungs clear left no time to argue. I was in need of urgent attention and any delay could have proved fatal. Fortunately, one of my lovely nurses used her initiative and went in search of a place to carry out my essential maintenance and discovered a quiet alcove just outside the lounge. There, partially sheltered from prying eyes, I endured the procedure I'd come to dread and waited helplessly for the suction machine to complete its vital but suffocating task.

To accommodate our party and equipment, the insurance company had arranged for the removal of nine seats from the aircraft and the installation of a screen to separate us from fellow travellers and provide some much-needed privacy. With so much medical gear in tow, the nurses needed time to get me settled and the airline agreed that we could board the plane thirty minutes before the other passengers. However, once again, our plans were interrupted by a bout of airport madness when a young man arrived at the boarding gate with an aisle stretcher that was filthy and totally unhygienic. My nurse sent him off to find a clean one but when he finally returned, his second choice was every bit as dirty and useless. We had been waiting in the departure tunnel for over two hours in temperatures that soared well into the nineties. The heat was unbearable and my stress levels were increasing by the minute. I felt trapped, not only by the furnace-like tunnel but also by my broken body which rendered me so utterly vulnerable and dependent. Once again the professionalism of the nurses looking after me took control and, in sheer desperation to get me on board without further delay, one of them took the stretcher away and washed it herself. After my experience, I couldn't help but think that employment at Orlando International Airport must require a high degree of bureaucratic lunacy.

As I was carried onto the rear of the plane, my blood pressure escalated alarmingly and the pain, despite my high level of tolerance, was excruciating. The discovery that there was no screen in place only added unnecessary humiliation to my suffering. I was laid on a cold metal bench that, without cushion or padding bench, pressed hard against my battered bones, making an extremely uncomfortable bed. The whole experience was a nightmare and I just prayed that time would pass quickly and it would soon be over. It was a horrific scenario and I didn't think things could possibly get any worse. However, an hour into the flight, I realised I was about to plumb new depths of misery when severe turbulence shook the plane with such force that, if it weren't for Paul and the nurses holding me in place, I would have been catapulted out of my makeshift bed. The stewardess's threat to report Paul to the captain if he didn't remain in his seat would have been laughable if it hadn't been so ludicrous. Apparently the airport's brand of lunacy wasn't confined to staff on the ground. Astounded, Paul couldn't be bothered to explain the effect a fall would have on me and why it was imperative I remain on the bench, even if that meant he had to physically hold me there. I guess like the nurse, he thought it was a case of stating the obvious. With a sigh of exasperation he told her to go ahead and file her complaint. Until the turbulence passed, he was staying with me. In the end, I was spared any further torture. The dangerous levels of my blood pressure, rising temperature, laboured breathing and indescribable pain left the nurses no choice but to sedate me for the rest of the trip.

We made a bumpy landing at Gatwick airport on the morning of Good Friday. I was relieved to have survived the flight and couldn't wait for the final stage of my journey that would bring me home. Regular airlines commuting between London and Belfast were unable to accommodate me, but our friend Max came up with a solution. One of his relatives, Mr Moore, worked in the offices of local minister and politician Dr Ian Paisley and, as soon as they learned of my plight, they arranged for a private air ambulance to transport me from London to Northern Ireland. Dr Paisley may be better known for oratory skills than rescuing damsels in distress, but I certainly owe him and his office a great debt of gratitude.

As I was carried aboard the air ambulance, my right hand clutched a tiny Easter bunny. My nurse had bought it for me during the long transatlantic flight and I truly appreciated her considerate gesture. No doubt she understood that after almost a fortnight where the only odour to fill my nostrils was the antiseptic smell of a hospital, the little bear's chocolate aroma was heavenly. Once on board I was in for another sensory treat. The pilot's familiar Belfast accent was a welcome sound to my ears and, for the first time since the awful accident, I heaved a real sigh of relief. I was finally going home. In sharp contrast to the long-haul flight, the short journey to Belfast International Airport was hassle-free and incredibly smooth. Our pilot, a young captain from Newcastle, was fantastic and went to great lengths to make our trip as easy as possible.

Once we landed, the plane taxied to a designated area where an ambulance waited to take me to the Royal Victoria Hospital. To our surprise and delight, we discovered that one of the paramedics was a friend of my brother's. I may have been battered and broken but I was so happy to be surrounded by familiar voices.

Mum was waiting for me at the hospital but as the doors opened and I was wheeled towards her, I heard her sharp intake of breath followed by the sound of her sobs. Nothing could have prepared my mum for the sight of her daughter's broken body and unrecognisable face. Life had already dealt her a raw deal but she never complained. Yet, despite her own pain and fear, Mum's first instinct was to try to alleviate mine. Gently she spoke to me, trying to reassure and perhaps infuse my traumatised body with some of her strength. At the sound of her voice, my tears started to flow and I knew she too was crying. The tube in my throat that prevented me from speaking had been a constant source of irritation but at that moment, unable to comfort my mum, I had never detested it more.

As doctors and nurses gathered round to assess my injuries, I could hear their exclamations of shock that I had not only managed to survive the accident but a 4,000 mile flight from America. I was desperately ill and needed the expert care of a hospital trauma unit. It was unbelievable that I had been discharged and allowed to travel in such a critical condition. Yet, money had proved the deciding factor and dictated my fate. Nevertheless, as I listened to the familiar accents that addressed me affectionately as 'love' or 'pet', I felt a surprising rush of gratitude to whoever had taken the decision to send me to my own country. American doctors had been wonderful and I owed them my life, but to be among my own people was a real joy.

Although medical teams in Tampa had already carried out a series of tests and X-rays, staff at the Royal Victoria Hospital decided to repeat the process. By the time I'd been scanned, examined and scrutinised, I was more exhausted than ever but the diagnosis was the same. I was lucky to be alive.

In those early days, when I was too ill for general visitors, Paul, Mum, Pop and my brother Ian took it in turns to keep me company. They brought me news from home, bits of chatty gossip and a few of my favourite talking books. But the best present was something that, until my accident, I'd always taken for granted. Permission to have a shower seemed like my birthday and Christmas had arrived at the same time! The evening before the big event, I was so excited and went to sleep dreaming of scented soapy bubbles and soothing jets of piping hot water caressing my body. By dawn, I'd had second thoughts and wasn't so sure that a shower was such a good idea. Instead of pleasure, I began to anticipate the agony that being moved would provoke. Still, I needn't have worried. With professional expertise and extreme care, I was transferred with the minimum of discomfort or fuss and allowed to revel in the warm soapy cascades.

Communication continued to pose a problem. My notepad was able to convey simple messages or requests but my questions were endless. I wanted to know everything about my condition and, more importantly, I needed to understand what the future held. How long before the wounds healed? When could I expect a return to some form of normality? The query that dominated my little notepad was always the same. How soon could they remove my breathing tube? The emergency tracheotomy had been crucial to my survival. Without it, the swelling around my larynx prevented air from reaching my lungs, shutting off my oxygen supply. Yet I hated the opening in my throat with a passion. It was uncomfortable, at times suffocating and the ritual of daily suctions soon became the horror of my day. Yet, at every reading of my pleas, doctors shook their heads, unable to comply. Until the swelling had subsided, I was stuck with the horrible little pipe.

Apart from the ability to talk again, I really looked forward to the day when I could give my taste buds a workout. A diet of bland high-protein drinks, syringed into my mouth several times a day, was less than appetising. I'm not a fan of milk at the best of times and within a few weeks was sick of the full-cream shakes laced with a selection of minerals and vitamins. Paul came up with an idea to give me a treat and add a bit of variety to the menu. Each day he arrived at the hospital armed with little jars of baby food and after heating them in the ward kitchen's microwave, filled a syringe and gently squeezed the puréed delights into my mouth. The taste of sweetened fruit was like nectar! Babies must have a wonderful time. I particularly loved the dessert 'strawberry fool' and always looked forward to the gooey treat. However, when Pop arrived with a packet of chocolate buttons and asked if I'd like to try one, I was beside myself with excitement. Eating one of the tiny chocolates was way beyond my capabilities but the tiny fragment that he did manage to slip carefully past the barrier of wires and into my mouth was indescribably delicious.

While doctors confided in Paul, they continued to keep their prognosis from me. During ward rounds, it was easy for them to avoid the subject. They didn't have to make eye contact and as I couldn't speak, the topic was neatly side-stepped. It was frustrating. However, when Paul started talking about changing the car, I felt the first stirrings of unease. Initially, I smothered the feelings with a layer of logic. Naturally, for the immediate future, mobility was going to pose a problem. Changing to a more suitable vehicle was the sensible option. But when he began suggesting we buy a plot of land and allow our friend Duncan to build us a lovely new bungalow, sparks started to fly. I realised that Paul, after listening to medical advice, had accepted that a wheelchair would always be a necessary piece of equipment and he had begun making plans to accommodate my long-term disability. If I could have voiced my feelings, I would have screamed. I may have to accept the restrictions that blindness imposes on my life but there was no way I was going to give up my mobility. I was determined that I would not spend my days confined to a chair. As shouting wasn't an option, I had to settle for pen and paper to make my feelings clear. While I scribbled furiously, Paul waited to read what I made of his suggestion. In huge bold letters I wrote: 'NO!! Believe me, my condition is only TEMPORARY!!' Smiling, he squeezed my hand, reassuring me that he'd got the message.

Chapter 16

Life in the Royal Victoria Hospital

Situated approximately ten minutes from the city centre, the Royal Victoria Hospital is among Belfast's most recognised landmarks. Fully equipped with state of the art technology as well as some of the world's finest medical experts, it enjoys a reputation second to none. It seems incredible that the sprawling complex of modern medicine began life in 1793 as a tiny fever hospital. With just six beds, it made little impact on the lives of suffering humanity, but by 1847 it was refurbished and enlarged to cope with an outbreak of typhus and cholera. Thirty-two years later, the granting of a royal charter added a touch of nobility to its title and the hospital became known as the Belfast Royal Hospital. By 1903, the premises had not only adopted Queen Victoria's name, but moved from Frederick Street in central Belfast to a much larger site on Grosvenor Road in the west of the city. As well as an impressive statue of the regal Victoria, sculpted by J. Wenlock Robins, the hospital claims to be the first building in the world to offer patients, staff and visitors the comforts of air conditioning.

Just over a hundred years after Queen Alexandra and King Edward VII officially opened the building, I too became part of the hospital's history when I added my name to their long list of grateful patients.

My world, once without physical boundaries, was now confined to a hospital bed. Yet I knew that just beyond my medical prison, life continued its hectic pace. A short distance away, the heart of Belfast city continued its frenetic beat as people, occupied with their individual dramas and dreams, hurtled through the day, unaware of the fragile nature of existence. They had no idea that, in an instant, plans can be thrown into chaos and life extinguished. It seemed incredible that just a few weeks previously, I too had been part of the complacent crowd of city-centre shoppers. Filled with excitement at the prospect of a visit to Buckingham Palace, there was nothing more worrisome on my horizon than the search for a perfect outfit and a pair of matching shoes. Suddenly, it all seemed so strange and remote.

The events of 29 March 2004 had changed everything, including my priorities. In the immediate aftermath of the accident, my only goal had been to stay alive, but as time moved on I began to take pleasure from even the smallest achievements. However, my first experience of sitting on a bedside chair proved both disorientating and embarrassing. After a month of lying flat on my back, sitting upright had promised a welcome change and I looked forward to the event. With gentle expertise, the nurses lifted me into the armchair, but less than ten minutes later the dizzying reality had me yearning to lie down again. Helplessly, I waited for one of the male nurses to put me back on the bed, but instead of easing my plight he only added to my discomfort by querying, in an unnecessarily loud voice, if I was waiting to use the commode. I was mortified. I knew the other patients could hear and, stung by his insensitivity, I grabbed my pen and wrote in huge letters: 'I AM NOT DEAF and NO THANK YOU!' I'd encountered this kind of ignorance before when people, equating lack of sight with an inability to hear, would shout at me. Sometimes, they even associated blindness with mental impairment and went to great lengths to carefully pronounce and enunciate words. Very often they would simply choose to ignore me, addressing Paul instead. More often than not, I saw the funny side and merely laughed at their lack of knowledge. Yet, when robbed of everything but the auditory senses and feeling acutely vulnerable, I resented this particular form of tactlessness.

It's amazing how quickly the body clock can adapt to the regulated pace of hospital life. Gradually, the morning bustle of doctors' rounds, followed by the lunchtime clatter of dinner trolleys and the buzz of visitors' conversations, became the sounds that measured my day. Whether it was a nurse wheeling me into the shower or Paul feeding me a syringe filled with baby food, I began to anticipate and look forward to every simple treat. The frivolities of life had been stripped away, leaving an appreciation that far outweighed the basic nature of the luxury. Equally there were periods in the monotonous schedule that I absolutely dreaded. The twice daily sessions of physiotherapy on my chest were hard enough to endure, but by the time the experts had finished torturing my poor arm and leg, I was totally drained. Nevertheless, as an elite athlete, I understood the value of stretching reluctant muscles and tendons, forcing them to co-operate and achieving their optimum levels of strength. I also knew that the amount of effort I put in would pay dividends later and made up my mind to accept that there was no easy route. Like anything that is worthwhile, regaining my health would require 110 per cent commitment. I simply had to get on with it. Still, there were many moments, especially in the days ahead, when pain threw me into such utter despair that determination and sheer willpower just didn't seem enough to get me through.

By its very nature, the hospital environment has its fair share of dramatic events. But, as far as patients are concerned, it can also be extremely boring and mundane. Once visitors leave, snippets of family gossip are passed around and shared like a box of chocolates. However, when Paul rushed into the ward one day, spluttering with excitement and clutching a letter, everyone knew they were in for an extra special treat. After all, it's not every day a girl gets a message from a prince! The previous year, I'd been invited to present the Gold Duke of Edinburgh Awards at Hillsborough Castle and during the event had been introduced to His Royal Highness Prince Philip. Apparently, after learning of my accident from Mr Eric Rainey MBE at the Awards Office, he decided to write and tell me of his sadness at the news and to wish me well in the future. I was ecstatic that such an esteemed gentleman should take time from his busy schedule to contact me. The considerate gesture not only made my day but provided an interesting topic of conversation for the whole ward, as nurses and patients teased me mercilessly.

Winning medals and world championship titles is bound to create a bit of a stir and I'd enjoyed a fair amount of time in the media spotlight. Equally I had grown used to locals in my nearby town of Lisburn stopping me in the street, determined to shake my hand and pass on their congratulations. I never ceased to be touched by these lovely expressions of support and encouragement. However, it began to seem that, even when immobilised in an intensive care unit, I was still attracting attention. At first, the arrival of an early morning visitor to the ward was of no special consequence. In an intensive care unit where patients' conditions can fluctuate rapidly, visiting times for next of kin and close family tend to be flexible. But when I heard the stranger approach and call me by name, I wondered what on earth was going on. Before I knew what was happening, he'd launched into an enthusiastic account of how he'd followed my career and had always wanted to meet me. He didn't seem to notice the inappropriateness of the circumstances, but the ward manager, who never missed a trick, came rushing over and, pulling the screens around my bed, gave him a severe tongue-lashing and sent him off. I didn't think much about the incident until a few days later when I received yet another missive courtesy of Her Majesty's Service. I couldn't believe my ears when the letter revealed the identity of my admirer. As well as charming a member of the royal household, I'd managed to add an inmate from Barlinney Prison in Scotland to my fan club. As the story unfolded I learned that the captivated prisoner had been granted compassionate leave to visit his mum who, like me, was a patient in the ICU of the Royal Victoria Hospital. Upon learning that his favourite water-skier was in the same room, he couldn't resist a quick introduction. Between a letter from the palace and one from jail, my presence in the ward certainly provided a lot of entertainment.

Physically, progress was agonisingly slow but I continued to revel in every minute triumph. My notepad, filled with requests, questions and messages, was fast taking on the proportions of a book. In fact, it's a miracle I didn't add writer's cramp to my list of injuries. To be honest, I don't think reams of scribbled, often illegible, words punctuated by a series of exclamation and question marks qualified as any form of popular reading material. At its best, the written word is a fantastic medium to convey the deepest thoughts, feelings and desires. But, disadvantaged by a lack of tools, not to mention a tendency to nod off mid-flow, my chances of producing a bestseller were limited, no matter how many pages I filled. Without a voice to lend expression and nuance, communication was confined to a few penned staccato type sentences. As an articulate woman used to self-expression, my inability to talk was unbelievably frustrating. I couldn't ask doctors about my condition, query treatment, or elicit a prognosis. With no input, I felt totally out of control. Even worse, I couldn't tell Paul how I felt. Somehow a scribbled 'I love you' doesn't have quite the same effect. Little wonder that the removal of the wires from my jaw and tube from my throat remained such important goals. As the weeks dragged on with no sign of realising either ambition, I began to wonder if I'd ever participate in a proper conversation again. Then, suddenly, out of the blue, I heard the magic words. The tube was coming out!

In reality, the process proved more complicated than expected. Unable to locate the internal stitches, it took several doctors and just as many days to decipher the handiwork of American surgeons and release me from my horrible pipe. While grateful to be free of the thing, I didn't appreciate the large hole it left at the base of my throat. Next to go were the wires clamping my jaw. Lying on the hospital trolley, heading for the department of dental experts, I naively assumed that with a few snips, my mouth would once again be wonderfully mobile. At that point, I'd no idea that the nightmare was only beginning.

After enduring thirty-two injections in my gums, I worried that with so much pain relief, my mouth might never recover any sense of feeling. Unfortunately, as it turned out, they were totally insufficient for the job in hand. When the nurse began cutting and pulling each wire through my tender and sensitive gums, I thought I'd faint from the agony. No such luck! I continued to feel every excruciating snip and tug. At one point, distressed and tearful, I begged her to put me to sleep but with oblivion denied, I had no choice but to endure the living hell for almost five hours. I just couldn't understand why it was necessary for me to go through such a horrendous experience. Surely, in our technologically advanced era, the procedure should not be so barbaric. Eventually the arrival of a doctor solved the mystery. My torture was not caused by some unavoidable but necessary medical practice. It was merely due to a pair of blunt wire cutters. If only the young woman had checked her equipment, I could have been spared the suffering. Long into the future I would wake up, drenched in sweat at the recollection of the incident. My only consolation was that, because of what I had endured, a nurse learned a valuable lesson and, hopefully, was able to spare her future patients the same intolerable anguish.

As days merged slowly into night, I began to gauge the passing of time by the slightest physical progress. The ability to stand on one foot, lie across a piece of medical equipment called a pulpit rollator and hop for a few paces, told me that I was one step closer to being discharged. Normally, the severe and extensive nature of my injuries would have required a long spell in a rehabilitation unit as the home environment wasn't equipped to deal with my specific needs. Apart from obstacles like stairs and steps, going home would mean I'd be alone for part of the day which, with a necessity for twenty-four-hour care, would be an impossible scenario. Paul's business demanded his presence and made no allowances for a badly injured wife. Yet, my family knew my desperation for familiar surroundings. They understood my desire to be where I belonged and were determined to find a way to allow me to recuperate at home. After talking it over they decided that, as Mum and Pop had taken early retirement, they would care for me during the day while Paul would take over the evening and night shift. Doctors and nurses may have supplied the medical expertise to rebuild my bones but it was my family who provided the love and support to restore my confidence and allow me to heal.

My diet of puréed baby food and protein drinks may have kept my body fed with essential vitamins and nutrients but they had done nothing for my figure. With a weight loss of over two stone, I not only felt weak but looked it. I was the proverbial example of skin and bone and every step left me feeling drained and exhausted. My broken left elbow required a special crutch and I couldn't bear to put any weight on my right leg. I was still a physical wreck and, at times, despair overwhelmed me. But I was alive and in better shape than anyone ever expected. I gritted my teeth and persevered, refusing to let this unexpected and unwelcome interruption in my life beat me. I would survive.

In the outside world my determination to push the boundaries may have earned me a collection of world records, but in the Royal Victoria Hospital all it got me was a stern lecture. A few weeks before discharge, I'd been moved to a side room where the relative quietness made it easier to sleep and, although I missed the general buzz of the bigger unit during the day, I enjoyed listening to my little talking machine. Engrossed in a thriller, I could temporarily find reprieve from the traumatic memories of the accident. However, privacy also had its drawbacks. Away from the immediate notice of nursing staff, it wasn't always easy to attract their attention. With patients whose conditions were always critical, prioritising each individual's needs was always difficult. On one occasion, my desire to visit the bathroom before retiring for the night happened to coincide with the ward's extremely busy schedule. After waiting for over an hour for someone to reply to my summons for assistance, I decided to use a bit of initiative and fend for myself. Carefully, I pulled the wheelchair close to my bed and gingerly lowered myself into it. Then, using my left leg, I slowly propelled the chair towards the bathroom, just a short distance away. I was jubilant. For the first time since the accident, I'd been able to experience a bit of independence. The little venture may not have warranted such an extreme sense of excitement and achievement but, for me, it was a huge milestone on my journey towards recovery. Delighted, I made my way back to my room, imagining the note of pride in Paul's voice when I told him what I'd accomplished. The sound of the staff nurse's voice interrupted my happy reverie and from the sharp notes, I could tell my escapade hadn't provided her with quite the same pleasure it had me. After helping me into bed and giving me the nightly dose of pain relief, she abruptly pulled up the cot sides, trapping me until morning. With a curtness that defied any reply, she informed me that I wouldn't be courting trouble on her shift and, banging the door on her way out, left me to ponder my errant ways. Nevertheless, despite the dressing down, I drifted off to sleep with hope in my heart and a smile on my face.

Finally, almost two months after my arrival, doctors prescribed their best medicine yet. I was going home. It's impossible to describe my sense of elation at the news. To the outsider, I would have appeared a perfect example of someone in dire need of a hospital bed. My face was still swollen, while my bones were held together by screws and bolts and, when not confined to my wheelchair, a specially designed crutch supported my shattered elbow. I certainly didn't paint a picture of health. Yet, as those closest to me knew, every step away from the brink of death had been a hard-fought battle. I may have been a mess but, so far, I had won. With the support of my family, doctors and friends, I was determined to conquer whatever lay ahead.

Chapter 17

Hell on Wheels

Driving through Belfast city centre can be slow at the best of times but in rush hour, traffic tends to come to a standstill. As Paul was collecting me from hospital on his way home from work, I knew to expect delays, especially as construction work was currently under way at the West Link dual carriageway. Yet nothing could dampen my enthusiasm. It didn't matter that the journey home would take a bit longer than usual. The prospect of sleeping in my own bed again was more than enough compensation for a few extra minutes of motorway madness.

A few days prior to my release from hospital Paul, armed with the dimensions of my wheelchair, went shopping for a new car. His choice may not have packed the same testosterone punch as its sportier rivals but, as it was practicality and not macho image that topped the list of essential features, the little Ford Fiesta ticked all the right boxes. I don't know how long Paul imagined I'd need the wheelchair-friendly transport, but I was determined it wouldn't be a permanent necessity. As events transpired, our relationship with the Ford Fiesta ended a lot sooner than either of us expected.

Strapped safely into the passenger seat, I listened as Paul described the long queue of stationary cars ahead of us and the rapidly forming one behind. It looked as though we'd underestimated the congestion. Already exhausted from the mere effort of sitting upright, I couldn't wait to get home and lie down. The first indication that I wouldn't be slipping between the sheets anytime soon was the sudden note of shock in Paul's voice followed by the words: 'Oh no! This does not look good!' Alarmed, I asked what was wrong but before he could explain that a lorry was hurtling at full tilt towards the cars behind, I'd already felt the impact. Incredibly, as we waited for the ambulance, the first piece of news I heard on our car radio was that due to a multi-vehicle pile-up on the M1 motorway, motorists should avoid the area. Sitting in the middle of a line of twisted metal, it certainly wasn't news to us!

Stunned by the collision as well as our unbelievable bad luck, I waited helplessly for paramedics to carry me into the ambulance and take me to our local hospital in Lisburn. Thankfully, X-rays confirmed that, apart from severe shock, no further damage had been added to my original quota. Much to Paul's dismay, his brand new Ford Fiesta wasn't so fortunate and, despite the mechanic's best efforts, didn't survive the crash.

Considering that on my journey home I'd been involved in a serious road accident, it was little wonder that, even in familiar surroundings, I felt strange and disorientated. Perhaps I'd equated going home with a return to some kind of normality but as the days passed I was confronted by daily reminders that my life would never be the same again. The last time I'd been in our home was the morning of my departure for Florida. I may have left the house weighed down with cases and skis but I hadn't a care in the world. I'd closed our front door, shivered in the chilly morning air and looked forward to my return when, hopefully, the springtime sun would have brought a little warmth. However, by the time I eventually came home, spring had already been and gone. The house had also witnessed a few alterations when, in order to allow Paul to manoeuvre my wheelchair, our good friend and neighbour, Gerry, had kindly installed ramps between the stone steps. Instead of using the front door, I had to come and go through our second level where, before reaching our bedroom and bathroom, yet another flight of steps had to be negotiated. It was sheer hell for me and very hard work for my family. Yet, regardless of minor alterations to our home, it was I who had experienced the biggest transformation. I'd gone to America a fit and healthy sports woman and returned with my face held together by eight plates, thirty-seven screws, a collection of wires, coral implants and a host of other surgical tricks to help rebuild bone structure. I had a Gamma nail holding my hip, femur and pelvis in place, while my shattered elbow bones were bolted together with pins. Pain from the physical injuries was torturous but the mental suffering was at times unbearable. Apart from nightmares that catapulted me back to the scene of the accident, forcing me to re-live the horror, I could not come to terms with life in a wheelchair. Paul may have been able to release me from the nightly onslaught by gently waking me but he could do nothing to give me back my independence. For the first time since losing my sight, I had to rely on Mum, Pop, Paul and Ian for everything. I can only describe that time in my life as hell on wheels.

Nevertheless, the human spirit is indomitable and in more optimistic moments, I could appreciate progress. For a start I could communicate, chat and even enjoy a few hearty chuckles with Paul. Eating remained a problem as only physiotherapy and time would eventually prise the stiffness from my jaws, allowing me a taste of real food. Still, I managed to find enormous pleasure in my ability to consume mountains of velvety chocolate mousse and creamy desserts without having to worry about putting on weight. I guess there's a positive side to everything, it just isn't always easy to find.

I attended the physiotherapy clinic at the local hospital several times every week. The painful sessions may have helped strengthen my body but when the physiotherapist told me that 99.9 per cent of people with my type of injuries never walk again, he came close to crushing my hopes. His warning that, in all likelihood, I would become yet another sad statistic was meant to spare me disappointment but the prospect of a lifetime confined to a wheelchair, dependent on others, was a powerful incentive to prove him wrong.

My initial attempts to climb the half dozen stairs to our bedroom took on the proportions of conquering Everest. Once I'd been helped from my chair, Mum went in front while Dad brought up the rear and, sandwiched between them, I, with the aid of crutches, hauled my broken limbs inch by agonising inch towards my goal. Many times exhaustion or pain overtook me and the expedition was abandoned, but on the occasions I managed to reach my summit, I felt on top of the world. Every day became an opportunity to move one step closer to achieving my new ambition. I would not allow the wheelchair to become a permanent fixture in my life; I was going to walk.

Within a few weeks, members from our extended family who had previously relied on phone updates from Mum or Pop were able to visit for brief periods. As much as I loved to see aunts, uncles and cousins, the effort of making conversation left me drained and in need of a nap. The BBC also contacted us to ask if we'd like to participate in a documentary that would, over a year, chart my journey towards recovery, eventually taking me back to Tampa General Hospital to meet the American doctors who had saved my life and rebuilt my face. I have to admit that initially I wasn't sure about the project. For me, appearing in front of a camera proved a particularly daunting prospect. Since losing my sight, I'd relied on memory to form the visual images of the faces of loved ones, as well as my own. Of course, I wasn't naïve enough to believe that the intervening decades hadn't left a few reminders that time was passing, but as far as I was concerned, the clock had stopped ticking more than twenty years ago, freezing us all in another era. Suddenly, I no longer knew how I looked. As well as shattering my face, the skiing accident had temporarily destroyed my sense of identity, triggering an avalanche of insecurities. Surgeons had done their best to restore my bone structure to its original proportions and, according to Paul and Mum, had achieved enormous success. Yet, in those early months, I wrestled constantly with uncertainties about my appearance. I knew there were many scars, as my sensitive and tactile fingers had traced every jagged inch. It took a long time and endless reassurances before I could accept that, despite having only a passport photo for guidance, Mr Halpern had indeed done a fantastic job.

Apart from the physical strain, I didn't know if I was up to the emotional demands of a televised documentary. Having a camera crew about the place for hours on end can, at the best of times, be tiring and intrusive. It wasn't an easy decision but in the end Paul and I agreed that the experience could prove therapeutic and may even help lay the ghosts to rest. The BBC's assurance that they wouldn't begin filming until I felt comfortable helped enormously.

As summer wore on, I took great delight in the outdoors. With so many scars, sunlight had to be avoided at all costs but sitting in the shade inhaling the flower-scented air was heaven. I was still on a lot of pain relief medication and even the smallest exertion left me exhausted but every day of life was a bonus. The fact that I had cheated death added a note of poignancy to my forty-second birthday and Paul wanted to give me an extra special present to celebrate. He hadn't a clue what to buy but fortunately, I knew exactly what I wanted. When Mum heard I'd asked for a puppy, she thought I'd taken leave of my senses. Her insistence that a young dog wasn't a good idea, especially in my condition, was understandable. I knew her reluctance was motivated by concern for my welfare but I really wanted to hear the patter of four tiny feet again. Since Toyah's death, I'd been too busy attending training sessions or competitions to even consider another dog. But circumstances had changed. Tentatively, I broached the subject with my physiotherapist, who told me exactly what I wanted to hear: a puppy was a great idea! There was no reason why being in a wheelchair should prevent me from having a canine chum.

It was probably a streak of cowardice that led Paul to bring the little creature home when he knew his mother-in-law was hundreds of miles away in Scotland! But I didn't care what anyone said; from the moment he placed her tiny form in my arms, I was in love. As the smallest of the litter, her timid nature had made her the target of sibling bullying and instinctively I wanted to protect and care for her. Running my hands over her soft, warm body, a name immediately sprang to mind and we decided to call her Angel. When Mum and Pop arrived the following week, Angel was sleeping contentedly in my lap. I waited, ready for Mum's tirade, but the only thing I heard was her sobs. Later, she explained how the sight of a helpless animal providing me with such comfort and joy moved her to tears. I was delighted that Mum, like me, had fallen for Angel's charms and from that moment the little dog became a valued member of our family.

The following months proved difficult in more ways than I'd imagined. Not only was I often housebound, I was increasingly lonely. While everyone thought Paul was handling the situation relatively well, in reality the accident had taken an enormous toll. Finding it hard to watch me suffer, he bought a new business and buried his grief in work.

Apart from the evenings, when he tended to my needs, we barely saw each other for almost a year. I knew he was in the throes of some kind of post-accident shock but I was powerless to help. In the early days, when my life hung in the balance, adrenaline had kicked in, erasing any thought of the future and enabling him to function in automatic mode. However, returning home had underlined the awful extent and long-term nature of my injuries, reinforcing the certainty that instead of a temporary interruption, our lives had been permanently changed. The accident had smashed more than my bones. Its painful ricochets had pierced the heart of the people I loved and there was no medical procedure to offer them relief. All I could do was wait and hope that time would eventually bring acceptance and allow my husband to heal.

While Paul was preoccupied with work, Angel was my constant companion. Interestingly, just as Toyah had helped me cope with the trauma of blindness, the little dog provided a source of comfort in the aftermath of the accident. She seemed to sense my limited ability as well as my mood and never got in the way but was always ready to offer a cuddle. I loved her to bits. I knew that Paul's immersion in work was a temporary coping mechanism and he'd soon be back to his old self. Meantime, I decided to focus on getting out of the wheelchair and back on my feet.

We'd known for some months that, in recognition of my services to disabled sports, I was to receive an Honorary Doctorate from Queens University in Belfast. I just didn't know when the ceremony would take place. When a letter popped through the letterbox telling me that graduation was scheduled for the following month, I was distraught. There was no way I'd be physically well enough to attend. The last thing I wanted was to miss such a prestigious, not to mention exciting, event. After talking it over with Paul, I decided I would accept the invite and wait to see what happened. Worst case scenario, I'd have to make my apologies and withdraw. However, if I did have to cancel, it wouldn't be from lack of effort on my part. The graduation ceremony proved a powerful motivation to get back on my feet and leave the dreaded chair at home. Over the next few weeks I pushed myself to the limit. Every day, after physiotherapy, I'd practise walking a few steps with only my crutches for support. Very often, I'd collapse either back in my chair or into bed, but I refused to give in. I was determined to walk to the podium in Queens University and deliver my graduation speech.

A few days prior to the actual ceremony, we were invited to attend a pre-graduate dinner. It was the first time I'd been to any kind of social function since the accident and I literally bubbled with excited anticipation. The dress code was formal but it didn't pose a problem. All I had to do was choose whichever of my dresses best fitted my new lightweight frame. I don't think, apart from my wedding day, that I'd ever been so skinny. I was determined that the wheelchair wouldn't form part of the ensemble and as high heels and crutches don't mix, my mum rummaged in my wardrobe and found a classy but sensible pair of flat shoes. As it turned out, my high expectations were totally eclipsed by reality when I discovered that my dinner partner was none other than the distinguished Senator George Mitchell. We had a fabulous evening and, although utterly exhausted, I fell asleep dreaming of American statesmen, champagne and music.

Within a few days, I was once again set for a night on the town! On this occasion, instead of evening attire I had to wear traditional graduation robes. My hairdresser, Julia, came to the house to cut and blow-dry my hair while, according to Mum, my beautician did a brilliant job of covering my scars. As I waited, ready to go, Paul gave me a hug and told me I looked every inch a beautiful graduate, and I knew by the catch in his voice that he was struggling to contain his emotion. The sound of my husband's pride was all the reassurance I needed. Unknown to me, in the days leading up to the event, Mum had been exercising some maternal muscle by ringing the university organisers, requesting that chairs be strategically placed along the route from my place at the dinner table to the podium. Aware of the effort it would take to make the journey, she wanted to make sure I had sufficient resting stages along the way. It was these constant displays of tactful consideration that gave me a fresh appreciation of how blessed I am to have such a fantastic family.

Finally, the moment for my 'walk' to the front of the Great Hall arrived. Leaning on two crutches, I struggled to my feet, hoping for an extra spurt of adrenaline to keep me moving. The podium, although just a short distance away, seemed out of reach. Yet, as the cameras began to roll, I kept going and before I realised it, I was standing in front of a microphone addressing my fellow graduates. I'd chosen the subject of 'learning' as my theme and, as I explained that the greatest lesson I had learned was the necessity to adapt to life's changes, I knew I'd hit the right note. The sound of applause was deafening. The gentle pressure of Paul's hand on my arm as we led the procession out of the Great Hall was reassuring but his whispered revelation that I had received a standing ovation was emotionally overwhelming. I don't think I have ever felt such an immense sense of privilege and honour. Mum and Pop were ecstatic. Not only had I made it safely through the evening, I'd achieved what I set out to do and once again refused to let physical restrictions limit my dreams.

Chapter 18

The Return to Florida

O n 29 March 2005, exactly a year after the accident, I was back in Florida and on my way to meet the strangers who had saved my life. Twelve months previously, I'd arrived at Tampa General Hospital alone and anonymous. In stark contrast, I returned surrounded by an entourage of media. I'm not sure what onlookers made of the cameras, lights and microphones; maybe they thought they had a celebrity in their midst! As part of the ongoing documentary, Paul and I had agreed that the BBC could film the reunion. Two weeks prior to leaving Belfast, we'd also given them permission to capture the gory details of the surgical removal of bolts from my knee. Thankfully, I was fast asleep and missed the whole show.

I didn't know what to expect from my visit to the American trauma unit or what emotions it would trigger. For the past year, I simply hadn't had the energy to cope with any psychological repercussions as I was too busy trying to recover from the physical ones. I rapidly discovered that the only way to deal with my feelings was to separate from them. Somehow the situation was easier to cope with when viewed from a distance. My family often remarked that when speaking about the accident, it was as though I was describing someone else's life. I think, in my mind, I was. While a skilled and professional counsellor can help to lead many trauma victims through their emotional jungle, I found it impossible to share my innermost feelings with a complete stranger and, after a short time, I as well as the poor counsellor was exhausted from the effort. Logically, I knew that the floodgates would eventually open, drowning me in torrents of anger or resentment at fate's cruelty. But in my fragile state such introspective analysis was too dangerous to pursue. The only thing that kept me going was an instinct for survival and a stubborn refusal to give in.

As well as the film crew, Paul and I were accompanied by television's popular sports personality Jackie Fullerton, who was to act as presenter of the programme. He was great fun and his easy banter managed to lighten the mood and bring a smile to everyone's face. Paul and I, as well as the rest of the team, thoroughly enjoyed his company. As I'd suspected, the process of making the documentary was often intrusive and difficult but over the months I'd built up a good rapport with the media crew, who by this stage had been at our home so often, they were practically part of the family! Undoubtedly one of the major bonuses of the project was the friendship that had developed between me and the programme producer, Karen Bowen. Her tact and sensitivity kept stress levels to the minimum while her constant encouragement at even the smallest physical achievement on my part proved a huge bolster to my confidence. I was really thrilled that, long after filming ended, Karen and I kept in touch and our friendship continued to blossom.

Our arrival in Florida certainly caused a bit of a stir but nothing like the commotion going on in my tummy. Yet I wasn't the only one experiencing a bit of emotional turbulence. As soon as the hospital came into view, Paul was bombarded by memories. I couldn't read the expression on his face but I knew by his sudden silence and tight grip on my hand that he was upset. Quietly I waited, unsure what to say and unwilling to intrude. I knew that Paul's time in Florida had been traumatic but I had no idea of the depth of his suffering. Naturally, he'd told me of his fear of losing me and his distress when lack of recognition had caused him to walk past my bed. He'd also spoken of the shock when nurses gently pointed me out. Yet, he hadn't found words to describe the profound loneliness that characterised his days as he sat in the hospital's garden and waited for news. Worst of all was the knowledge that my husband had been staggering under a heavy burden of guilt. It didn't matter that the feeling was irrational and unfounded. Paul's logic was simple. If he hadn't introduced me to the sport, I wouldn't have been in Florida and the accident would never have happened. Undoubtedly his reasoning was a natural response to shock but the flaw was obvious. Without his encouragement to participate and share in the fun of water-skiing, my life would have lacked so much passion and joy. I never would have known the thrill of pitting my skill against other talented skiers on an international level and walking away with the coveted title of World Champion. Instead of allowing blindness to confine or define me, Paul had given me the opportunity to find the freedom of success. Listening to the pain in his voice, I instinctively wanted to put my arms around him and wipe away the hurt, but the proximity of cameras, not to mention a couple of crutches, got in the way and it grieved me that there was nothing I could do. Doctors had often remarked that my pain threshold was extraordinarily high but when it came to dealing with my family's anguish, my tolerance level was zero.

While it was the sight of the hospital building that triggered Paul's responses, it was the smell that activated mine. Once inside the doors, my nostrils were filled with the antiseptic odour that is characteristic of all clinical environments and immediately I was transported back in time to the days when every conscious moment revealed yet another new agony. With rising panic, I recalled the feelings of fear when, unable to see or speak, I had tried to make sense of the unfamiliar surroundings and the events that had brought me there. To be honest, my initial instinct was to leave immediately and catch the first flight home, but Jackie Fullerton, with acute recollections of his own recent spell in a cardiac unit, empathised completely with my aversion to the hospital aroma and was able to calm me with a measure of sympathetic support.

As soon as we entered the trauma unit, I began to recognise the mechanical sound of artificial life support. The constant hiss and bleep of the hi-tech equipment that, in those early weeks, had provided me with a bridge between life and death, unearthed memories I thought I'd forgotten. For a second, the progress and triumphs of the past year disappeared and I was back to the days when, after a lifetime of battling for independence, I was reduced to relying on the expertise of strangers and a battery of machinery for every breath. Whatever the expression on my face, the cameras couldn't capture the kaleidoscope of horror that played out in my mind.

However, amidst the sound of fear there were the unmistakable voices of kindness. One by one, I was introduced to the people who had worked tirelessly to save me. Dr Lewis Flint, the first of the trauma team to make my acquaintance and assess my condition, told us how my severe loss of blood, comatose state and rapidly failing heartbeat had led him to believe that death was imminent. Dr Rodney Durham, trauma surgeon, took up the story and went on to describe the long, painstaking hours of surgery required to reassemble my mangled bones. Listening to the gruesome account, I began to develop a fresh appreciation of what my family had endured. Every day, while my comprehension had been dulled by anaesthesia or sedatives, Paul, Mum, Pop and

Ian had been confronted by the stark reality of my awful injuries.

Apart from the doctors' more technical details, it was lovely to hear the voices of nurses Celeste, Sabrina, and Christine, who had with such dedication tended my every need. Their genuine delight at my progress was touching but their surprise at my height made me laugh. After two weeks of viewing me in a horizontal position, they'd no idea I was so tall. Despite the many individuals who came to offer their congratulations and encouragement, there were two people I desperately wanted to meet. First on the list was Dr David Halpern, the surgeon who had given me back my face.

We caught up with him at his private clinic and, although light-hearted and jovial, his greeting was incredibly poignant. After an enthusiastic 'Great to see you again Paul,' he turned to me and, taking my hand, asked, 'and who might you be?' It was such a moving moment, I could have cried. My first encounter with the doctor had been as a woman without definition of cheekbones, nose or eye sockets. It is impossible to describe the shock of losing what is in essence, the outward expression of identity. But as a woman, the eradication of my features was the ultimate blow to my sense of femininity and self-esteem. What female could not appreciate the depth of such a loss? Regardless of mood, the face is the mask our gender presents to the world. With a few coats of mascara, a dab of blusher and a hint of lipstick, we camouflage our insecurities or fears and prepare to meet each day. Without the façade, our vulnerabilities are exposed and open to hurt. I could never thank Dr Halpern enough for rebuilding my bone structure and restoring my face. The patience and kindness he had shown to Paul the previous year when, over a cup of coffee, he'd attempted to explain the intricate nature of my surgeries, was just as evident during our meeting. While the cameras rolled, Dr Halpern examined every inch of my face with all the enthusiasm of a craftsman delighted by his handiwork. With the inspection complete, he took time to answer my questions, reassuring me that, despite the many surgeries ahead, I was on the road to recovery. It would be a long and painful slog but then, I'd travelled the route many times before and its painful brambles held no surprises. Speaking with Dr Halpern not only allayed a lot of my fears but helped fill the gaps in my memory, especially the one where he explained why he'd chosen such a complicated method to wire my jaws!

During my stay in the Tampa Hospital, I may not have absorbed the finer details of Dr Halpern's medical jargon but I would never forget the kindness of the nurse with a magic cap! I couldn't wait to meet the woman known to me as Jessica and thank her for the best shampoo I'd ever experienced. Throughout the day I'd listened for her voice and was disappointed to have missed her. However, once filming had ended, Paul made some enquiries and we were told that Jessica couldn't come to meet us as she was currently in the neo-natal high dependency unit of the hospital. No doubt any newborn would have been fortunate to have such a devoted and skilful nurse, but Jessica's presence among the tiny infants wasn't as a hospital employee. She was there in the role of a mum. Paul and I were taken to meet her and her premature baby who, weighing less than a 2 lb bag of sugar, was stubbornly clinging to life. Looking at the soft contours of the baby's face, Paul remarked that while he may not be able to detect any family resemblances as yet, he definitely knew a fighter when he saw one! As well as the opportunity to offer my congratulations, it was lovely to meet and thank the woman who had shown such understanding and female empathy. In return, her sincere affection and delight at my progress was one of the highlights of our visit.

The kindness and co-operation of hospital staff was amazing. Even the helicopter pilot provided the camera crew with a take-off demonstration identical to the one he'd made on the day he was summoned to my rescue. Before leaving Florida, I was invited by Kelly, the hospital educator, to have my photo taken for the hospital's Trauma Hall of Fame. Apparently, I was to join the line-up of survivors who, despite the circumstances, had proved that even when hope has gone, life is stronger than death. I've no doubt that there are many prestigious and famous photographic collections in the world but few are as inspirational as the ones that adorn the walls of the Tampa General Hospital. Apart from individual stories of traumatic events, the images are a testimony to the human spirit's capacity for overcoming catastrophe, as well as its determination to survive. I considered it an honour to be counted among such courageous company.

My return to Florida had certainly opened many emotional wounds but it also brought closure to a part of my life that, for the past year, had haunted my dreams. Paul had always done his best to answer my questions but, blurred by shock and time, his memories were often sketchy and failed to satisfy my demands. As we boarded the plane for home, the BBC were happy with the material for their documentary while Paul felt relieved that he'd been able to share some of the emotion he'd kept hidden for so long. Apart from a few doggie souvenirs for Angel, a bottle of perfume for Mum and a couple of keyrings for Pop and Ian, the best thing I took away from Florida were the missing pieces in the jigsaw of my life.

Three weeks after our return from America, I was back in hospital for yet another instalment in an endless chain of reconstructive surgery. I never got used to the constant round of operations followed by painful weeks of recovery. However, there was one area of my life that was rapidly developing into an enjoyable routine! As well as the BBC documentary, I had agreed to make a programme with Ulster Television for their series known as 'A Day in the Life.'

Its inspirational theme was meant to offer encouragement and motivation but when we turned up for filming, I couldn't resist a bit of fun. The programme presenter, Claire McCollum, is also a friend of mine and, as well as making the experience as easy as possible, I knew she'd be up for a laugh. Filming was due to take place at our ski club Meteor and when Paul and I turned up for the initial shot of us driving into the car park, we had to wait out of camera before our cue to drive into focus. Paul parked the car behind a nearby hedge but, as we waited, a bit of devilment got into me and a mischievous plan began to hatch. Paul, recognising the note of impish excitement, asked what I had in mind. I explained that it would be a fantastic prank if it was I and not he who were seen to be driving into the parking lot. Naturally, the idea appealed to his zany sense of humour and, as fast as crutches would allow, we changed seats. I could barely keep a straight face when, at the presenter's signal, I began to inch the car slowly forward. With Paul's instructions to move a little to the right or turn slightly to the left, I drove with a deadpan expression towards the crew. Paul's description of the cameraman's puzzled expression as he swung his lens first from passenger then to driver was more than I could take, and in the end I was laughing so much that I couldn't continue. Everyone shared in the joke and we all fell about in hysterics. We did eventually get the programme wrapped up but not without many such incidents of light-hearted fun. There's no doubt that throughout my journey towards recovery, I've encountered numerous bleak moments where I thought I'd never see the light at the end of the tunnel. There have been countless obstacles that at times have seemed insurmountable and I've lain tearful and exhausted by my attempts and failure to overcome. But equally I have discovered that, even in the darkest times, the sun does shine. The ability to laugh in the face of difficulties is not only a gesture of defiance, it is the best medicine for every ailment. As my life unfolded, I began to think, if I didn't laugh, I'd probably go mad!

Chapter 19
The Ultimate Buzz

December 2005 sprinkled its usual brand of festive magic throughout Northern Ireland. As a rash of Christmas trees spread across the Province, Paul and I shared a chuckle at the memory of the miniature version that had, in our first home, seemed more of an ornament than anything else. A couple of house moves later, the additional space ensured that its successors were of much larger proportions and enjoyed a prominent display in our living room. More importantly, they provided Santa with sufficient room to get a few extra presents under the branches! Yet, regardless of the many beautiful trees that decorated city centres and homes, for the pupils of Downshire Primary School, it was the one in their school grounds that proved a special source of interest. Planted by Her Majesty Queen Elizabeth during the official opening of the building in 2005, the little Himalayan birch would remind future generations of their very important guest. Unlike its County Down neighbour, Belfast may not have entertained royalty but for the thousands of fans who packed the Odyssey Arena to hear bands Oasis and Coldplay perform, the city certainly wasn't short of excitement.

I can't recall what I got for Christmas in 2005 but I know it wasn't fun! Recovering from yet another instalment of major surgery, I spent the day curled up on the sofa trying to block out the pain. My decision to remove the Gamma nail that American surgeons had used to bolt my femur, hip and pelvis had taken a lot of soul-searching. But I knew that while it remained in my body, I could never build up sufficient muscle to allow me to walk unaided. I may get rid of the wheelchair but for the rest of my life I'd have to rely on a crutch. As medical props didn't feature in my plans, I was determined it too would have to go. Apart from a desire to walk unaided, I was also concerned that a future fall may cause the bones to shatter around the Gamma nail, consigning me permanently to a wheelchair. Nevertheless, it wasn't a decision to be taken lightly. After quizzing my physiotherapist and doctors, Paul and I weighed up the pros and cons and, although I knew the recovery period would be tough, I thought the benefits would outweigh the disadvantages. But there was a moment when, on the day of the operation, the surgeon's graphic account of what I could expect almost made me change my mind. His pessimistic prognosis of an eighteen-month recovery period, a lot of which would be spent in a wheelchair, indicated a setback rather than progress. Noticing my pallor, he left me to think things over and promised to return later for my answer. Immediately I rang Paul, hoping for some positive encouragement. But there are some decisions that have to be made alone. Naturally Paul was sympathetic but he couldn't give me the answers I wanted. Dr Philip Glasgow, chief physiotherapist with the Sports Institute, came up with some good advice when he told me to trust my instinct and, if I decided to proceed, he and his team at the Institute would work with me to make sure I achieved the best results possible. While hospital physiotherapists were fantastic, I wanted more than mere mobility and I knew that if anyone could help me attain peak physical condition, it would be Philip Glasgow and his incredible team of physiotherapists at the Sports Institute Northern Ireland. As an elite athlete, I'd already experienced what their knowledge and dedication could help me achieve. When the surgeon returned, I was still apprehensive about the operation but I was adamant it should go ahead.

Past experience had taught me that, apart from taking the medication, the only remedy for post-operative agony was time. I would just have to wait for my body to come to terms with the shock of the recent onslaught. Doctors had already warned me that I would never be totally free from pain and would have to learn to manage it, but the possibility of walking unaided made everything else pale in comparison. I would endure whatever punishment my body demanded if I could only walk. As I lay on our sofa, listening to the sound of Christmas carols on the radio, I stroked Angel's fur and allowed myself to dream, although somehow the secret images in my mind didn't correlate with the ambition I'd spoken aloud. Instead of walking through city streets, the vision that would have given Paul a coronary but brought a smile to my face was of me slicing through the water on my favourite slalom ski. I knew that competitive skiing had gone forever but if I could have asked for one Christmas wish, it would have been for an opportunity to get out on the water.

Like all who suffer chronic pain, I had good days and really horrible ones. In a more positive frame of mind, I was able to focus on the goal ahead and concentrate on rebuilding strength in my limbs. But at times, the agony was unbearable, sapping my energy and reducing me to tears. In some of these darker moments, I was overwhelmed by grief for the enormity of my loss. I couldn't make sense of the direction my life had taken and was plagued by the simple but unanswerable question that every frightened and hurting human hurls towards the divine observer: 'Why?' Yet, no matter how many times I asked, there was no reply. To say I never plunged into the depths of depression would be untrue but I was never submerged for long. Perhaps my ability to fight against the murky current was simply due to genes that had programmed me for survival. Maybe it was a reluctance to put my family through any further suffering. Yet I believe that heaven could not ignore the thousands of petitions that ascended on my behalf.

As 2005 drew to a close, Paul and I welcomed the New Year from the comfort of our living room. Joking, we shared our individual resolutions and we both laughed at my announcement that I intended to take part in a future marathon. As Paul pointed out, I always did set my sights high. I didn't dare tell him that I wanted to ski again! That would have been a step too far. His revelation that he intended to keep a closer eye on me in 2006 did cause me a bit of concern. I knew that since the accident Paul had found it difficult to trust anyone other than family to take care of me when he wasn't around and, while I understood his fears, I didn't want to be limited by them. I'd tasted freedom and I was determined that, once I'd overcome the physical restrictions, I'd grab every opportunity for independence.

Mary Peters may hold the official title of Dame but as our friendship grew, I christened her with the affectionate label of Auntie Mary. Her pragmatic and fun-loving approach to life was often the tonic I needed most and as she was a regular visitor to our home, Paul also developed a great respect and fondness for her. As patron of the Springhill Hospice in Rochdale, Mary had been asked if she could bring along an inspirational speaker to their annual dinner which was due to be held in May 2006. I'd done a lot of this kind of work during my involvement with Social Services and later in my role as chairman with Disability Sports Northern Ireland. I'd always enjoyed the experience and felt a real sense of achievement at the thought of helping others to accept and move on from some traumatic event. Granted, at the time, many of my themes were educational as I attempted to inform society at large about the needs of the visually impaired community. When Mary asked if I'd go along and speak at the Rochdale event, I agreed immediately. Ironically, since my accident, I no longer thought in terms of simply overcoming blindness. Experience had taught me that it isn't the particular incident or trauma that matters. It is how we as individuals cope with the aftermath that will eventually determine our quality of life. Apart from such an interesting speaking engagement, I knew that the weekend would be a lot of fun and, with such a trustworthy chaperone, Paul was equally happy to let me go. With Auntie Mary around, there was no way I'd get up to mischief.

It had been almost six months since surgeons removed the Gamma nail and I was slowly regaining my strength. The dreaded crutch was still a regular companion but I knew that by persevering with my intense physiotherapy programme, I would eventually be able to ditch it.

I was so excited at the prospect of speaking at Rochdale and took ages deciding what to wear but as with the graduation ceremony at Queens, I had the problem of finding something that actually fitted. Regardless of my consummation of endless jars of baby food and chocolate desserts, I just couldn't gain weight. In the end I settled on a full-length pale lilac dress with sparkling ear-rings and necklace to match. My shoes, although a shiny silver, were, as usual, sensibly flat but the crutch was as drab as ever.

At Rochdale the dinner went extremely well and by the time I stood to address everyone I hadn't a trace of nerves. As I outlined the story of my life, there was a hushed silence but I have to admit that, at the mention of my impromptu search of a policeman's legs while trying to find the doorway to Marks and Spencer, the place erupted in laughter. It was a lovely evening and I couldn't believe my ears when, at the end

of my talk, I was given a standing ovation. That evening I
made a lot of new friends and, through Mary, became
involved with the Springhill Hospice. That evening, as I lay in
bed replaying events in my mind, I began to realise that life
was leading me on yet another adventure. Glaucoma had
taken my sight but it wasn't able to steal my determination or
passion. The accident had broken my body but it would
never break my spirit. Regardless of what fate threw in my
path, I would simply change direction and set new goals.
Competitive water-skiing may have been beyond my
capability but in time, I was determined to get back on the
water. Meanwhile, I would use my knowledge and experience
to equip and help others reach their full potential. I fell asleep
to the sound of appreciative applause but whether it was for
my ability as an inspirational speaker or a world champion
skier, I don't know—yet I was happy just the same.

The weekend at Rochdale was packed with various events
but on the Sunday morning, Mary and I had a few hours to
fill before flying home. As we were only a couple of miles
from my home club in Britain, Whitworth Water-Ski Centre,
I couldn't resist the opportunity to pay my team coach Andy
a visit. Accompanied by Ken and Joan, the lovely people who
were looking after us, Mary and I set off to say a quick hello.
We arrived at the centre and while the others tactfully
disappeared for a short stroll, I waited at the top of the
walkway for Andy. As soon as he spotted me, he leaped from
the back of the boat and onto the dock, and came running to
enfold me in a huge hug. Andy hadn't seen me since the
accident and couldn't believe the progress I'd made or how
well I looked. It was so lovely to hear his voice again and I
couldn't wait to bring him up to date with all the news.

As we sat in the clubhouse cradling mugs of tea, I told him
of the horror of the past two years. He listened quietly as I
recounted the gruelling operations, painful physiotherapy,
traumatic flashbacks and sleepless nights. Occasionally my

voice faltered as I tried to express the awful devastation of losing my face. But as well as the darker threads that ran through my life, there were also many glints of happiness and fun. I couldn't help but laugh as I explained about the fan who had come all the way from a Scottish prison to make my acquaintance. Yet, as the pattern of sadness and humour unfolded, I couldn't help but notice that my family's care and support was woven beautifully through it all. For a few moments neither of us spoke. Listening to the birdsong outside, my thoughts immediately turned to a topic familiar to us both: skiing conditions on the lake! It was a lovely day and I knew the water would be fabulous. When I commented that it was cruel of fate to tempt me with such perfect skiing conditions, I couldn't believe Andy's reply. For a second I sat stunned, wondering if I'd heard him properly. Could he really have invited me to ski? When he repeated the question, I knew I should have refused but oh, the prospect of being back in the water was too tempting to refuse! Before I could think about it, I agreed and waited while Andy dashed off to find me a wet suit.

It was barely six months since the Gamma nail had been removed and my bones were still hollow and fragile. The last thing I needed was a fall. But, I knew that if I didn't grasp this opportunity, it might never come again. Of course there was an indisputable element of risk and I'd no idea if my body was up to the challenge. Yet, the circumstances couldn't have been better. I trusted Andy both as a professional and a friend and knew he'd never suggest anything he thought beyond my capabilities. I was also extremely familiar with the layout of the lake and was confident there were no hidden dangers.

Over the past couple of years, every task had seemed laborious and slow. But changing into that wet suit appeared to take no time at all! Kitted out and ready to go, I stood in the clubhouse waiting for Andy to lead me to the dock, when all of a sudden the door opened and Mary Peters stood there, her voice incredulous with shock. Immediately she launched into a tirade, giving me a real telling off. I listened as she lectured me about the madness of even contemplating going out on the water, and my explanation that I trusted Andy didn't have the calming effect I'd hoped for. I couldn't help but feel a little guilty when she pointed out that Paul trusted her and she felt responsible for my safety. Unable to find the words to explain that this was something I really had to do, I simply pleaded for her understanding and reassured her that everything would be fine. As for sharing my intention with Paul, well, apart from lack of time, there was no point in worrying him. I decided I'd cross that bridge when I came to it. Linking my arm through Mary's I suggested she join Andy on the boat to watch me ski. At first I thought she was going to explode but to her credit, she knew when she'd lost the argument and reluctantly agreed. Our friends Joan and Ken were equally fearful and while Joan decided to join a tearful Mary in the boat, Ken couldn't bear to watch and went for a walk instead.

Lowering myself into the water, I was shaking so badly I didn't even notice the icy temperature. Barely able to grasp the rope I began to wonder if my elbow, never mind my fragile hip, could take the strain. Suddenly, doubt crept into my mind, stealing my confidence and making me wonder if I really had taken leave of my senses. But, it was now or never. If I didn't seize this opportunity, I may never ski again. Once back in Northern Ireland, I would not only have to battle against medical opinion but would have to fight my way past the protective barriers that Paul had erected around me. One by one, I chased the negative thoughts, ignored my trembling hands and, assuming position, shouted the familiar command 'Hit it!' The boat surged forward, the rope stretched taut and I was off. How can I describe the feeling of sheer delight as my body once again responded to the familiar movement of the water, the slalom ski beneath my feet or the wind in my face? To say I was happy could never do justice to the emotion that coursed through my veins. The smell so peculiar to open water and fresh air proved a heady mixture as it filled my nostrils and assailed my senses. I was ecstatic. Eventually, physical weakness overcame me and I had to signal to Andy to return to the dock. As my coach hit the boat horn in a triumphant blast, I climbed out of the water, exhausted but jubilant. Mary was the first to greet me and it touched me deeply to hear her crying. Yet, as she hugged and congratulated me, I knew that my friend's tears were prompted not by fear but joy as she shared in my moment of success. Ken and Joan, apprehension forgotten, added their voices to the chorus of delight.

Back at the clubhouse, Andy went to scrounge some soap and shampoo so that I could shower the smell of the lake from my hair. But as I stood beneath the hot soapy bubbles, nothing could wash away the smile from my face.

On the return flight to Belfast, Mary, although happy for me, fretted at what Paul would make of my escapade. With a promise not to tell him until she was at a safe distance, I gave her my word that I'd wait until he and I were alone before spilling the beans. Paul met us at the airport and couldn't wait to hear all the news of our trip to Rochdale. No doubt he put Mary's hesitant replies down to fatigue but when she left us to make a quick phone call, I grabbed the opportunity and blurted out my guilty secret. For a moment, Paul's silence suggested that this time I'd gone too far and was in serious trouble. Taking his hand, I tried to gauge the extent of his fury. To my astonishment the expected explosion didn't come. Instead of an angry eruption, Paul quietly asked what Andy had made of my performance and whether I had enjoyed the experience. I told him that my coach had been impressed and that I was overjoyed to be able to ski again. As my husband drew me into his arms, I knew he understood what the event had meant to me. There wasn't a lot of conversation but then Paul isn't a gushy sort of guy. By the time Mary returned, she knew by the smile on my face and Paul's happy grin that I'd confessed and found absolution. Climbing into the back of the car, she breathed a sigh of relief and with a 'thank God that's sorted' settled back for the journey home.

Chapter 20
Living the Dream

The trip to Whitworth certainly provided my friends with a day to remember. No doubt it also played havoc with Dame Mary Peters' blood pressure. Even today the memory of me skiing round the lake, holding onto the rope with one hand and waving to her with the other, is enough to set her pulse racing. Yet, despite her concern for my safety, when it came to praise and encouragement, Mary's generosity knew no bounds.

Unfortunately, Dr Philip Glasgow wasn't as understanding or impressed. I may have been on cloud nine when I returned from Whitworth but the next morning brought me back to earth with a bump when I awoke stiff, sore and barely able to move. Slowly, I showered and dressed, wondering if Philip would notice my extra-tender condition. Any thought that I'd be able to hide the pain, and more importantly the reason for it, vanished immediately when Dr Glasgow noticed me hobbling gingerly along the clinic corridor, and he demanded to know what had happened. His guess that I'd taken a tumble was a reasonable assumption; after all, who would have believed the truth? I didn't want to keep anything from the experts who had been so good to me yet neither did I want them to douse my dreams. But in the end I had to confess that, far from having fallen, I'd actually managed to remain upright and ski round a lake! Philip was at first incredulous, then furious. Firing one question after another he demanded to know if I had at least used two skis. Sheepishly, I had no choice but to admit that my sporting adventure had taken place on my mono slalom ski, although I did try to soften the blow by adding that it really was the safer option. With two skis, there was the danger that one might catch the other, pulling my legs in different directions and leaving me in an undignified split. The explanation didn't have the desired effect and, to my horror, I heard Phil call my orthopaedic consultant at the hospital and tell him what I'd done. I couldn't hear the exact conversation but there was no doubt that Mr Eames was equally shocked and angry. Lying on the clinic bed, I let the tirade wash over me. Naturally, I understood the doctors' reaction. I had taken a risk that could have ended in disaster but, when weighed against what I stood to gain, I knew I'd done the right thing. It wasn't simply a case of knowing I could physically ski again. My brief adventure had not only given reality to my dream but provided a focus for the future. The road towards recovery was slow and painful but now I had a purpose to make it all worthwhile. Gradually, his anger faded and Dr Glasgow's voice adopted a tone of grudging admiration. I could hardly believe my ears when he said that as I was so determined to ski again, he and Dr Eames would help me achieve my ambition, provided I adhered to their ground rules. The list sounded endless but I didn't care; I'd do whatever it took to get back on the water and ski again. If I could do that, then there was a good chance I'd be able to get my life back.

I launched into the rehabilitation programme with renewed enthusiasm. Phil and his team of physiotherapists, as well as my consultants, kept their promise and gave me the benefit of their medical expertise as well as their encouragement and support. In fact I owe them all an enormous debt of gratitude.

The next time I slipped my feet into my skis, it was with the blessing of my physiotherapist and medical consultants. My family may have been a little apprehensive but they knew how much it meant to me and, apart from a warning to be careful, said nothing to dampen my spirits. Initially, as agreed with Dr Glasgow and his team, I stuck to a basic routine and used two skis to simply ride around the lake, building up strength and confidence. In the gym, I gritted my teeth against the punishing schedule designed to encourage bone growth and concentrated on the prospect of getting back to normality. As the summer wore on I was able to get up on my mono slalom ski followed by a precarious but successful attempt to use the one designed for tricks. My hollow bones were gradually filling out but it would be at least eighteen months before they'd be strong enough to allow me to even try to jump. In between the hours in the gym, at the clinic or out on the water, I spent many in a hospital operating theatre as one painful surgery followed another. Instead of anticipating or dwelling on each procedure, I learned to tick them off one at a time before focusing on the next. I was like a blinkered horse, refusing to be distracted from the path ahead. As far as I was concerned, there was only one way to go and that was forward.

Over the months, Andy, the team coach, had watched me grow in confidence and was impressed by my progress. I too was pleased at how far I'd come but when I learned that I'd been selected to join the team for the 2007 World Championships due to be held in Australia, I was stunned. Simply getting back on the water had been an ambitious dream, but to take part in competitive skiing, especially at world class level, had never entered my mind. I wasn't sure if my body was up to the challenge but if Andy, aware of my physical limitations, was happy to have me onboard, there was no way I'd pass on the opportunity. Whether or not the medical experts or my family had reservations about the wisdom of my participation, no-one voiced an objection. Perhaps experience had shown them that, once I'd made up my mind about something, there was no talking me out of it. Instead, they joined forces and gave me their utmost support.

The championships were due to take place in May and Andy decided it would be a good idea for the team to spend the winter training in Florida. I could not believe that I was returning to America as part of the British team of water-skiers. It was such a contrast to the last time I'd visited when I'd barely been able to walk the corridors of Tampa General Hospital. Paul may have joked that his decision to accompany us was to make sure I stayed away from trouble. But I knew his real motive. Concerned that the experience may trigger too many traumatic memories, my husband wanted to ensure I had a familiar shoulder to cry on.

We left Northern Ireland at the end of January and arrived in what should have been a subtropical paradise but, as luck would have it, the region was experiencing one of its worst winters in decades. With a severe frost in the morning, not to mention a biting north wind that left our teeth chattering, we spent the whole time trying to keep warm. I don't think I have ever been so cold. None of us had anticipated the freezing conditions and had packed our suitcases with hot sunny days in mind. Locals must have thought we were mad when we turned up at the shops hoping to buy more appropriate clothing. Florida's reptilian population were also feeling a trifle let down by the weather and, in a desperate attempt to find warmth, they climbed onto the top of the ski ramp hoping to soak up whatever feeble rays were available. I was so glad I was not going to jump. The thought of landing with a huge snake dangling from my ski was too horrific to contemplate.

The Swiss Ski School is a gorgeous purpose-built centre with ski lakes and golf courses but we all accepted an invitation to remain at a friend's house nearby. Getting back into the water in Florida was more difficult than I expected and I battled to control the awful tremors that shook my body every time I stepped into the lake. I was so cross with myself for allowing the sensation of fear to get the better of me. But even the reminder that Paul and Andy were with me to keep me safe didn't lessen the panic. Eventually, I realised that there was nothing I could do about my body's traumatised responses, and I decided to let the feeling wash over me before focusing on the task ahead. It wasn't easy but, at every training session, I steeled myself for the physical onslaught, waited for it to pass and then got up on my ski and did what I was out there to do.

There wasn't a lot of time to prepare for the 'Worlds' and after training in Florida we headed for the British-run Extreme Gene Water-Ski and Wakeboard School near Cordoba in Spain where Matthew Southam, top world coach, put us through our paces. Thankfully, the weather was a great improvement on Florida's big freeze and we settled down for two weeks of training in lovely warm sunshine. As the reservoir is forty metres deep, anchoring a jump ramp proved a tad difficult and our practice was confined to slalom and tricks. Any free time was spent in the tiny village where I was able to put my language skills through their paces. Noticing that I was blind, the manager of the local hotel asked if our party was on holiday but when I told him we were the British Disabled Water-Ski Team, he merely laughed, thinking I was joking, and said it wasn't possible. By the end of the week, word had spread and both the villagers and the Spanish manager had seen us on the news and realised that physical or sensory disability does not impair skill, talent or success.

In the weeks leading up to the 'Worlds' event, individual team members had made arrangements to continue training abroad, which meant that instead of travelling to Australia as a unit, we would make our own way to the competition venue. On this occasion Paul stayed at home while I arranged to meet my team-mate Michael, a wheelchair user from Scotland, at Heathrow airport and fly together to Singapore, where we'd stay overnight before catching a flight to Sydney. Since the accident, I found sitting or standing for long periods painful and exhausting, and the journey was an absolute nightmare. Nevertheless, we arrived at our destination in one piece and settled back to await the others and recover from the flights.

After a week of acclimatisation, things finally got under way. The tournament, due to be held on a river that was filled with fresh water crocodiles, turtles and snakes, promised skiers a few hair-raising moments. But for me, the biggest fear wasn't the wildlife, although the snakes did make me shudder; it was the prospect of going over the ramp. I still wasn't convinced my body was ready for it. It was eighteen months since the Gamma nail had been removed and the doctors were pleased that healing had gone according to plan. I'd come so far and endured more than I'd ever imagined and the last thing I wanted to do was jeopardise all the hard work. My mind continued to conjure up a lot of reasons why I shouldn't jump but in all honesty, I was just plain scared. I decided to ask the coach if I could do a dry run and simply ski past the ramp on the first lap of the lake, but his gruff retort that I was a champion and not a beginner left me in no doubt that it wasn't an option. I'd either have to go for it or quit. As the latter had never featured on my list of solutions for life's problems, I knew I'd be going over that ramp.

Accelerating towards a huge ski ramp at speed must be a scary prospect for a sighted person. But, believe me, lack of vision doesn't lessen the fear. In order to test my body, I decided that for my first set, I would jump at just 1 metre. As I approached the ramp, adrenaline kicked in and the next thing I knew I was sailing effortlessly over to land safely on the other side. Thrilled that I'd not only conquered my anxiety, but that my body had suffered no ill effects, I increased the jump height to 1.25 metres. Naturally, I knew my physical limitations and would not push my luck. It was fantastic to be participating at such a high-profile competition but, as my coach had assured me, there was no pressure to achieve anything dramatic. It was just great to have made it so far. Nevertheless, I couldn't help but feel for the team when I learned that our biggest rivals in terms of countries like America and Australia were competing with a full quota of fourteen members. We could only afford to bring a small group, consisting of just seven skiers. I knew that for Team GB to retain the top team title, every one of us would have to give the performance of our lives. No, there was certainly no pressure!

As I waited on the dock, ready to compete in the slalom prelim, I could not believe the reality of the situation. Despite my vast reservoirs of optimism, I think that two years ago even I would have baulked at any prediction that I'd ever compete at any level of competition, never mind the 'Worlds'. My thoughts were interrupted by the announcement that I was next to ski.

Once out on the water, I was in my element. It felt so good to be doing what I'd always done best, but when I returned to dock I learned that my scores weren't the greatest. It didn't matter; none of the others had achieved fantastic results either. When the results were announced, I was thrilled to learn that I'd actually won the slalom prelim.

Tricks came next and there was no doubt I'd given the best performance. I managed to score the world record and won my team valuable points. It was incredible and I was on a real high. If this was a dream, I didn't want to wake up.

So far, slalom and tricks prelims had gone in my favour and given my ego a tremendous boost but I still had to jump.

Making my way to the dock, I did my best to remain calm, although the butterflies in my tummy took no notice whatsoever. I knew that my fear of the ramp was linked to the accident and the only way to sever its hold was to get out there and keep jumping. I might feel the occasional panic but it would not dominate my life. Whatever problems I anticipated on the water, I hadn't expected them to take place even before I'd left the dock. Just as I was about to participate in the jump prelims, I slipped my feet into the skis only to find that both bindings had split. After spending the past three years stored in our garage at home, the rubber on my skis had dozed and on contact with the warm Australian water had softened and come apart. Aware of the rule applying to equipment failure on the dock, I knew I had three minutes to make things right or face immediate disqualification. The unexpected emergency certainly took my mind off pre-jump nerves! Shouting for our team manager and coach to bring some duct tape from my bag, I waited while they quickly strapped the bindings around my feet. Thank goodness they finished within the allotted time, but as I skied off I couldn't help panicking at the thought of what would happen should I fall on landing, as I knew my tightly taped bindings would not release me on impact. It was a scary prospect and I found it impossible to jump with my usual confidence and managed only average scores. But, I did win!

The final audio slalom event took place at 7.30 a.m. During my absence from the sport, this particular discipline had changed and the course now had a wider angle. Some of the skiers compensated for this by flicking the rope on the turn, sending a tremor down the line and triggering the device sooner and at a shorter angle. This put them at an unfair advantage and I couldn't understand how judges failed to notice or curtail the practice. I'd had nightmares about the final audio slalom event but by the time I left the dock to run my first pass, I was amazingly calm and focused. The second pass went just as well and when I completed the course and skied home, I had achieved a score of 5.5 buoys at the top speed of 55 kph and set a new world record. My team was equally delighted when they picked up the additional points. In the tricks final, I managed to hit the record and once again gave my team a reason to celebrate.

By the time the jump final arrived, the guys had patched up my ski bindings with a borrowed punch and a few zip ties provided by Alan Murray, one of the World Council members from Scotland. The result felt a lot more secure and lent me a new confidence that enabled me to land every jump and achieve 95 per cent of the world record. Once again, our team was happy to benefit from the extra points. Throughout the event, the river banks had been lined with spectators and journalists who clapped and cheered my success. It was an incredible feeling as people rushed to shake my hand and congratulate me, not only for my water-ski performance but for overcoming such a major hurdle in my life.

Three years after the accident, my body still required major surgery and an intensive rehabilitation programme. I had accepted that physically I would never be the same again. Every day would bring a new challenge to overcome or a pain to endure. To those who knew me best, my will to survive appeared as strong as ever. But I knew it had changed. The spirit of determination that had helped me battle blindness now had a different character. Three years of fighting my way back to life had honed and sharpened its mettle, leaving it stronger than ever. Four water-skiing titles, including the overall world, and five gold medals had earned me recognition as a world champion, but for me, they also told another story. Each hard-won success was a testimony to the fact that, if we want them badly enough, dreams can come true.

I had gone to Australia with nothing but a determination to try, and I left a champion. Despite what life had thrown in my path, I had made it back to the top of my profession. The applause of my team, who had also won the 'team title', as well as that from rival competitors, totally overwhelmed me. I was also surprised and delighted to be singled out as one of the top three skiers of the tournament and was chuffed with the presentation of a Silver Overall Skier award. There were many congratulatory messages from around the world but the best had to be from Paul when, in a rare display of emotion, he commented that if it was up to him, he'd give me a bucketful of medals as I'd always been and always would be a champion.

Chapter 21
Moving On

The only word to describe my mood on leaving Australia was euphoric! It wasn't the first time I'd returned home as World Champion but I don't think any of the previous three events had tasted quite as sweet. All of my titles and medals had been earned by hard work and self-discipline, but those achieved at the 2007 World Disabled Water-Ski Championships had demanded even more. They were the result of single-minded determination, sheer physical agony and indefatigable optimism. Yet, as I carefully packed the evidence of my success, I was acutely aware that the victory did not belong to me alone. The victory was shared by the amazing teams of medical experts both in Tampa General Hospital in Florida and the Royal Victoria Hospital in Belfast. Equally my friends and physiotherapists at the Sports Institute Northern Ireland deserved an enormous portion of applause. On a more poignant note, the shiny medals and impressive titles were a tangible reminder of the unconditional nature of my family's love.

I couldn't wait to be back in Northern Ireland but as the return journey required a stopover in Bangkok, Michael, my team-mate, and I decided to fit in a quick adventure. We'd heard about a river taxi service that offered a guided tour of the little shanty houses and temples that lined the muddy banks and decided it would be an interesting experience. When we arrived at the jetty, I immediately sensed Mike's hesitation to climb aboard and when I asked why he didn't want to get into the boat, he replied that if I could see the state of it, I wouldn't want to either. Even worse if Paul was here, he'd go mad at the thought of me perched on top of a grimy cushion in a boat that was unbelievably filthy. As I never had allowed my husband's reservations to get in the way of a perfectly good exploit, not to mention the fact that we'd already paid our fare, I cajoled and persuaded Mike until he eventually joined me in the little craft. It wasn't until we were paddled out into the river and I heard the ominous creaks and felt the water lapping at my feet that I began to wonder if Mike had been right all along. Maybe it wasn't such a good idea after all. As we moved further downstream, the stench of the water was overpowering. I listened in amazement as Mike described the precariously stilted homes where families and neighbours jostled for space while children waved to us as they played and splashed in the river's polluted water. In stark contrast to the scenes of deprivation and squalor, the landscape was peppered with ornate and lavish temples as well as luxurious hotels where wealthy tourists strolled through beautiful manicured lawns, impervious to the suffering a short distance beyond. I was so touched by the poverty of the people and felt such a sense of gratitude for the blessings of my life that when a canoe of local merchants arrived and offered to sell little trinkets and ornamental elephants, I bought the lot. My purchases may have made little difference to the river people's lifestyle, but they certainly provided me with a reminder of the many privileges I've enjoyed.

Our brief stop at Heathrow airport gave me an opportunity to call Paul and confirm the time of my arrival. I was completely shattered from the trip but when Paul told me that some of the media would be waiting to meet me, I decided to make myself presentable with a dab of lipstick and a change of kit. Thank goodness I'd made a bit of an effort. As I stepped off the plane at the George Best Belfast City Airport, I was flabbergasted to hear the roar of applause and shouts of congratulations. The place was packed with journalists, television crews, friends, family and well-wishers. Taking my hand, Paul led me through the crowds who cheered and called their delight at my success. In Australia, I'd experienced a lot of media and local interest but nothing could compete with the warmth of the welcome I received from the people at home. All over Ireland, individuals from every walk of life and both sides of the community had taken an interest in my welfare as well as my career. They had showered me with cards, flowers and words of encouragement, urging me on towards recovery. It was a privilege to be the object of such dedicated interest and I was thrilled to bring them a reason to celebrate. Stopping to chat and accept thousands of good wishes, we made our way slowly towards the exit. Leaving the airport took almost as long as the flight to get there! But I didn't care—I felt I had achieved the impossible and it was wonderful.

The year 2007 was magical. It didn't seem that I could be happier. My return to the sport of water-skiing, especially in such a dramatic way, was more than I could have wished. Apart from the titles and medals in Australia, the year also contributed a host of fabulous honours to my treasure chest of memories. The British Water-Ski Federation World Champion Award was a lovely surprise, as was the overall trophy for Lisburn Sports Personality of the Year Award. Winning, for the fourth time, the Belfast Telegraph Sports Personality with a Disability Award was overwhelming but the icing on the cake was receiving the Titanic Achievement Award, which is only presented to five people on a five-yearly basis for what is described as 'Titanic Success'. At last I had made it. My life was back on track and I was moving, apart from when surgery de-railed me for a week or two, full steam ahead.

After Australia's glorious sunshine, the summer at home was a complete washout. Constant heavy rain caused water levels to rise and within days our clubhouse at Meteor was flooded. In fact, weather conditions were so extreme that the British National Disabled Competitions had to be postponed. It was frustrating but there was nothing anyone could do. It's a common misconception that, as getting wet is part and parcel of the water-skiing sport, rain doesn't matter. Yet nothing could be further from the truth. A heavy downpour, especially when driven by strong winds, can blind skiers as well as the driver of the boat. The best way to describe the sharp impact of the stinging sheets of water is to compare it to a session of severe facial exfoliation.

With skiing temporarily suspended, I decided to turn my attention to an aspect of the sport that had been bothering me ever since my return. The audio slalom system, designed by computer genius Chris Mairs, who was also a member of the British Visually Impaired Team, took vi skiing to new levels. Affectionately known as the 'Bat Blaster' by those who enjoy a healthy disregard for political correctness and admit to being as blind as a bat, the system was invaluable. Used correctly, it could enable blind or visually impaired competitors to learn to slalom ski in the same way as their sighted contemporaries. The only problem with the Bat Blaster was that it left too big a margin for cheating. I'd encountered the practice in Australia when skiers used a flick of the wrist to trigger the sensor and score the buoy. Apart from the unfair advantage, it concerned me that if nothing was done to correct the fault, the overall standard of slalom skiing would eventually drop. Frustrated, I called a meeting of all the vi classified skiers and their coaches. After bouncing around a few ideas, it was agreed that, as I was an elite athlete with the Sports Institute Northern Ireland, I should contact the University of Ulster and make an appointment to express our collective concern to one of the sporting officials.

Within days, I had a meeting with Dr Nigel Dobson, Director of Sport, and was delighted when, after listening to my explanation, he suggested we work together to find a solution. Not only could our joint efforts help improve audio slalom skiing but they would provide the university with an ideal project to enter in the '25K Competition', an event similar to the popular television programme 'Dragon's Den'. Meetings between the various departments were rapidly arranged and before long I was spending my days immersed in the intricacies of mechanical and electrical engineering. It was a fascinating experience to work alongside such competent and dedicated professionals. With a combination of their scientific skill and my knowledge of the problems of skiing blind, we came up with quite an amazing system. Technically, the device is based on the use of infra-red sensors and, although primarily for visually impaired skiers, has much potential in the skiing community as a whole. Competitively, water-skiing is still relatively a minor sport but as a recreation, it enjoys huge worldwide interest. The device, a virtual slalom course, requires little more than a boat and a clear stretch of water for a novice skier to learn the rudiments of slalom. Our aim was to test the device rigorously on water before submitting it to the World Council, who would hopefully approve and adopt it for future tournaments. To date, the team has encountered numerous teething problems but we're hopeful of success in the near future. As an innovative project, our device was among the top ten entries in the '25K Competition', and although we may not have stolen the show, we did make it to the finals and were delighted to learn we had taken first place in our category. It certainly provided us with a good enough reason to celebrate.

The pattern of my life was, and will continue to be, woven with some very dark and sombre shades. Simply getting out of bed in the morning will always be a long and painful process as I go through the ritual of exercising and stretching my rebellious limbs. The severed nerve endings in my face act like an uncomfortable anaesthetic to my skin, making me feel as though I'm a reluctant patient trapped forever in some mad dentist's chair. Every evening the routine of massaging uncooperative muscles in order to induce sleep has always been time-consuming and tedious. The crushing of lymph glands as well as my tear ducts doesn't stop me from crying but it does prevent drainage of fluid, which has necessitated the nightly ritual of running an electronic wand over my face to stimulate blood flow and hopefully reduce swelling. Sometimes, I long to jump into bed, curl up and listen to my talking book. I miss the mornings when, as soon as the alarm went off, I'd bounce up, throw back the covers and greet the day with energy and anticipation. Despite being blind, I'd moved through life at a hectic rate. Those simple pleasures have gone forever. Reconstructive surgery has intruded relentlessly as surgeons have done their best to return bone structure and define and enhance my features. Nevertheless, even the blackest threads only serve to highlight and accentuate the numerous splashes of vibrant colour. My zest for life may on occasion lose its lustre, but it has never faded. The absolute joy of skiing has remained brilliant throughout the design, while my marriage to Paul runs luminous and gold from beginning to end. Like many things, it's only when viewed from afar that I have found the perspective and balance to enable me to appreciate how fortunate I have been.

While the Australian and Spanish sunshine helped ease my aching bones, Northern Ireland's damp and cold climate only added to the problem. By November 2007, I was experiencing a lot of additional discomfort so, as a treat, Paul decided that it was time for the whole family to take a break. To everyone's surprised delight, he arranged for Mum and Pop to accompany us on a trip to Prague. There was just one tiny, furry problem. My parents usually looked after Angel when Paul and I were away so we needed to find another reliable sitter and there was none better than our friend and dog breeder, Michelle. I was confident that Angel would have a great time, getting spoiled and making new chums. We set off expecting a week of family relaxation and fun. What we got was a holiday from hell. The weather in Prague was an icy minus four degrees and our feet were frozen as we braved the blizzards, trying to make the best of things by visiting all the local sites of interest. But it wasn't the snow or freezing temperatures that brought the trip to an abrupt end and sent us home numbed with shock. It was a phone call from Michelle's husband Tom telling us that my lovely little Angel was dead. An attempted burglary at our breeder's home had resulted in the security gate being forced open, allowing several of the dogs, among them Angel, her mother, grandmother and another champion of the toy poodle breed, to escape. Disorientated by the unfamiliar surroundings, the little dogs had fled into the road where they all met their death. When Paul broke the news to me I was devastated. It just didn't seem possible that the tiny bundle that had given me so much comfort was gone. In the early days when I was confined to a wheelchair, Angel had sat on my lap, offering the odd sympathetic lick of my hand or nuzzling my face. Later, when I was struggling with crutches, she had trotted behind me, making sure never to get in the way. To the outsider, she was merely a pedigree dog but to me, she was my baby and I loved her. Inconsolable, I wept for the empty space in our home as well as my heart.

I knew that replacing Angel would be impossible but when Michelle called to tell me that the poodle's sister had given birth to twins and would I like to visit them, the answer was a definite yes! Once again, as I cradled the sleepy pup and ran my hands over her soft woolly body, I was smitten and agreed to take the little female home. We called her Hollie and she rapidly became part of the family. However, a few weeks later, when we returned to visit Michelle, Paul and I were so touched at Hollie's delight to be reunited with her sibling that we ended up taking them both home. When I rang Mum to tell her about the latest addition, I laughingly reminded her of the time when, at just sixteen years of age, I'd persuaded her to come with me to a fortune teller. Like many teenagers, I couldn't wait to hear what fate had in store for me. The mystic's prediction that twins were definitely a part of my future was spot on but there was no mention of woolly coats, wet noses or eight spindly legs.

With torrential downpours and icy winds, the summer of 2008 was a repeat performance of the previous year. In fact, if it hadn't been for the calendar's confirmation, I would have sworn we were stuck in a time warp. The forecast didn't offer much hope of change but the prospect of competing in the British Disabled Nationals, which were taking place at my home club in Whitworth, managed to dispel some of the gloom. Apart from taking part in the event, I looked forward to meeting old friends and catching up on the latest news. Paul's decision to come with me was an extra bonus as, no matter how big the crowd, his cheers always seemed to sound the loudest.

Standing on the dock, my hair plastered to my head and rain running down my face, I waited to ski. I was cold, damp and thoroughly miserable. Yet, despite the horrible conditions, the elements didn't affect me as much as they did other skiers. Apart from Northern Ireland's climate, I was used to everything from old boats to large, uneven wakes. Finally, I skied off for the slalom final and hoped for the best. Beginning at 49 kph, I ran my first pass, then the next and the next. I couldn't believe it, I was on a roll. First I ran down the rope shortenings and after completing a 13 metre pass, prepared to try it at 12 metres. My best score in practice was four buoys at a rope length of 12 metres, but when we shortened it to 11 metres I knew there would be hardly any wake to cut through. The chance of scoring any buoys was miniscule but, to my amazement, I actually scored three buoys with this incredibly short leeway. Breaking the record by thirty-three buoys was, for me, a once in a lifetime experience that I could never repeat as there simply wasn't enough rope remaining. With a grin from ear to ear, I revelled in the cheers of team-mates and rival competitors, who joked that as I'd been out on the water so long, I should pay a double entry fee. Paul, bursting with pride, caught me in an enormous hug that almost lifted me off my feet. I knew I had given the performance of my life and I was ecstatic. Every agonising moment of the past few years found its worth in that rare moment of triumph and I knew my painful investment had finally paid dividends. It was just my luck that the rain had put the video cameras out of action, ensuring that the only way to replay the dramatic action was with memory recall.

Still, as Paul and I joined the team for a long and well-deserved celebration, it didn't matter. Long into the future we would remember the day that Janet Gray pushed physical endurance and sporting skill to the boundaries and reached far beyond anyone's expectations.

Chapter 22

The Fire

My success at the Nationals seemed like a good omen for the European competitions, which were due to be held at Recetto in Italy, about an hour's drive from Milan. Other cities in Italy may find fame in cultural or artistic heritage, but Milan is renowned as the fashion capital of Europe and while my priority was to bring home as many shiny medals as possible, I hoped to find enough room in my case for a few trendy Italian bargains.

Originally, my friend had agreed to accompany me and act as guide during the tournament but two days before we were due to leave, she rang to say that she'd had a slight fall and wouldn't be able to go after all. I understood her decision but it did leave me in a bit of a pickle, as finding a substitute at such short notice would be practically impossible. Paul, with a heavy work schedule, simply couldn't afford the time off and I began to worry that I'd have no choice but to cancel. In the end, my mum stepped in and saved the day. I was truly grateful to her for helping out but I also thought the break would do her good. She'd never been to a tournament and I'd no doubt she'd enjoy the experience. Pop was equally happy for Mum to tag along and, as he's a fantastic cook, we knew he wouldn't go hungry. If only we'd known what lay in store!

We set off to catch an early morning flight to Manchester, where we had arranged to meet up with my team-mate Steve, who was also blind. I have to say that with Mum's family history we couldn't have wished for a better or more experienced guide. After an uneventful journey, we arrived at Malpensa airport in Milan and began the daunting search for a taxi large enough to accommodate us as well as our bulky equipment and baggage. Before long, a taxi driver approached Steve and asked where we wanted to go. At first I thought my ears were playing tricks on me but there was no mistaking the familiar voice and accent. 'Sergio!' I cried. 'Is that you?' His delighted response was the only confirmation I needed. 'Hey sweetie, you remember me?!' he shouted, rushing over to embrace me in an enormous continental hug. Standing outside Milan's airport in a city where everyone was a stranger, it was unbelievable that I'd bumped into one of my oldest friends. I'd first met Sergio many years ago in Denmark when he was the Italian team's coach and I was making a very nervous debut to international water-ski competitions. No longer involved with coaching, Sergio had traded the waterways for the much more dangerous pursuit of manoeuvring his way through Italian traffic. With his own taxi firm, he had proved that whatever the route, he was destined for success. Bundled into the back of his spacious cab, Sergio and I reminisced, laughed and traded news while he drove us safely to the Busola Hotel where, after helping us unload our gear, he wished us luck and kissed me goodbye, leaving me to wonder when or if we'd meet again. It was such a lovely coincidence that brought back so many happy and nostalgic memories.

The following day was Friday and, as the rest of the team weren't due to arrive until Saturday morning, Steve and I decided to begin training immediately. Accompanied by

Mum, we set off for the Recetto Ski Club, where we had a great time zooming round the lake, perfecting tricks and cutting back and forth across the wakes. After all the exercise and fresh Italian air, we were ravenous and looking forward to a delicious dinner at one of the local restaurants. With Steve on one side and me on the other, Mum led us back through streets where the savoury aroma of garlic and onions drifted from open doorways, tantalising our taste buds and whetting our appetites further.

The sound of emergency sirens may vary slightly from one country to another, but the meaning behind the shrill scream is always the same. At the unexpected commotion and noise, I turned to Mum, waiting for an explanation. She described the crowd of onlookers, journalists and television crew who milled around, eager to witness the evening's unexpected drama. Several fire engines were also parked outside the hotel and security officials had blocked the entrance to the street. The momentary note of concern in her voice disappeared immediately when she learned that the fire was confined to the little supermarket next to the hotel and that we were in no danger.

At around 1 a.m. we, together with the other guests, were permitted to enter the hotel lobby, although firemen insisted we wait in the lounge while they, as a precautionary measure, searched the upper floors. As it was after midnight and officially my birthday, there was no point wasting an opportunity for an early celebration and I decided that everyone should join me in a glass of wine. By the time firemen arrived to give the all clear, we'd had a great time and made a lot of new friends into the bargain, but it was proving difficult to keep our eyes open and we couldn't wait to climb into bed and drift off to sleep.

With Mum leading the way, we made our way to the fourth floor where she and I were sharing a room, while Steve stayed in the one next to us. Just as I'd finished my stretching ritual and eased myself between the lovely cool sheets, I heard the fire alarm go off. Mum immediately bounced out of bed and ran into the corridor to find out what was happening, but within a few minutes she'd returned to tell me it was a false alarm and nothing to worry about. Apparently a member of the hotel staff had explained that the sensitive device had been triggered by smoke from the fire next door and there was no need to panic. Relieved, we settled down to dream away what remained of the night.

Despite exhaustion, we found it difficult to doze off as the smell of smoke was becoming stronger and the air felt heavy with fumes. I suggested that we turn off the air conditioning system as it was probably responsible for blowing the pollution into our room. As I climbed out of bed, Mum told me not to bother, the electricity had just gone off and the air conditioner was no longer a problem. By this stage, Mum and I were coughing a lot and breathing was becoming more difficult. Before we could figure out what to do, a fireman was banging on our door and shouting that we had to get out immediately as the hotel was on fire. It was my worst nightmare. I'd always feared being trapped in a fire, unable to see or find my way to safety. Thank God I had my mum. For a moment, as the fireman stood in our room, screaming instructions, I was overcome with a weird sense of illogic thought that reminded me of the time when, as I lay bleeding to death on a ski dock in Florida, all I could think about was making sure the paramedics didn't cut my shorts off. Once again, my mind had sought and found refuge from shock in the irrelevant and banal. As the hotel burned around me and the air grew dense with smoke, the thing that bothered me most was that there was a strange man in our room and I was wearing my birthday suit! Fortunately, the strident note in Mum's voice as well as her order to 'move it' had me into my pj's in no time at all and, as adrenaline took over, I remembered to collect our passports and money from the safe. On our way out, I grabbed the first two coats I could find, despite the fact neither one belonged to us.

With the fireman holding my arm and leading the way, Mum and I made our way down the hotel stairs. The fire escape was already in flames so our only option was to try to exit via the main doors. We knew that security staff had already been to Steve's room but as we descended through thick clouds of choking smoke, I began to panic for my friend's safety. I had no way of knowing where he was and, in the pitch black, Mum couldn't see anything or anyone in front of us. Immediately, I began screaming his name and, from somewhere below us, his voice drifted up the stairwell, reassuring me that he was okay. I almost fainted with relief as I knew that, like me, Steve would be terrified of fire. After what seemed an eternity, we reached the ground floor and spilled, choking and gasping for air, into the fresh and wonderful smell of an Italian dawn. Steve was there to meet us and as we hugged, we heard the sound of cars exploding in the hotel's basement. Within seconds it was followed by the terrific din of windows shattering in the heat and smashing all around us to send dangerous shards of glass flying into the street. Unable to see, Steve and I stood motionless together, confused by the chaos. Yet, with Mum holding each of us by the hand, we knew she had brought us to a safe distance and we were in no danger.

Later, huddled on park benches, wrapped in warm blankets and sipping from bottles of cool water provided by the emergency services, we waited for transport to another hotel and reflected on our lucky escape. If we had fallen asleep, the smoke would have silently filled our lungs, making certain we never awoke.

As Mum described the beautiful shades of purple, gold and scarlet that streaked across the Mediterranean sky, we finally arrived at our temporary accommodation, everyone secretly glad to discover we were sharing a room. This was not a time for any of us to be alone. The three tiny beds were far from luxurious but as we lay quietly chatting, our occasional silence punctuated by the distant screech of sirens, we believed we were the luckiest people on earth. Steve and I didn't voice the thought but we both knew that a human tragedy had been narrowly avoided. If the fire had started on Saturday night instead of Friday, the hotel would have been filled with twelve teams of physically disabled and sensory impaired competitors, making it impossible to get everyone to safety.

The following morning, the full story unfolded. The fire had indeed started in the adjoining supermarket but it had quickly spread through the underground car park and up into the hotel building. Fire fighting crews did their best but it was impossible to save the Busola. Fortunately in human costs, the damage was limited to casualties suffering from smoke inhalation, although I did feel sorry for the German cyclist who, unable to find alternative accommodation in the town, had booked into the hotel and lost his bike in the fire. Filled with gratitude for our escape, it wasn't until we returned to our room that the practicalities of life began to intrude. For a start, I didn't think I could walk around the little town of Novara dressed in skimpy pj's and a pair of flip-flops without attracting attention. There was only one thing to do; we'd have to go shopping! Fortunately, I'd rescued passports as well as money so we should at least be able to buy toiletries and a change of clothing. Unfortunately, it was August, the European holiday season, and everywhere, apart from a tiny store in the centre of town, was closed. At home, I'd always taken such care of my appearance and would never have set foot outside the front door unless colour co-ordinated and fully presentable. But desperate situations call for the proverbial desperate measures. There was nothing else for it; I'd have to go to town wearing a pair of sunglasses and my pyjamas. Mum's assurance that no-one would notice temporarily bolstered my confidence but as she led me through reception, out of the hotel and into the street, a horde of waiting reporters told me that half the world was about to witness the spectacle. As the cameras clicked, I could hear Mum trying to stifle a sudden fit of the giggles. It was a ludicrous situation. As journalists began firing questions about the full extent of the incident, I suddenly realised that Paul and Pop would be listening at home. Naturally we'd called and told them about the fire but, not wanting to worry them, we'd played down its seriousness. Mum and I would wait until we were safely home before telling them that our hotel had actually burned to the ground. In a bid to introduce a lighter note, I turned the conversation towards my inappropriate dress code and joked that the fire had been caused by one too many candles on my birthday cake.

With the arrival of the other teams, my attention rapidly turned towards the competition. The Recetto Water-Ski Club, also home to the Water-Ski Federation, is a fantastic ski site that incorporates three purpose-built lakes, while the continental sunshine and lovely warm water make it a popular venue with many skiers. As preparations got under way, conditions were perfect and I looked forward to enjoying the event. Initially, audio slalom caused the usual bit of wrangling and disagreement but, as one of the judges had already declared my skiing to be fine during practice, I was happy enough. On the day before the competition officially began, skiers were given a final opportunity to perfect their individual tricks. I set off around the lake, confident and familiar with my technique as I went into the final one, known as 'a wake back to back'—which basically means that I begin in a backward position and cut into the wake to do a 360 degree turn in the air before landing to face in the same backward direction. There was nothing different about the trick and I'd performed it several times before. However, on this occasion I landed a little off balance and toppled over. It was such a minor fall and didn't appear serious enough to those watching from the boat to warrant pulling the trick release that would detach me from the craft. Nevertheless, as I fell, my hand slipped inside the handle of the rope and I ended up being dragged painfully along behind the boat. The sharp tug of the rope tightening around my wrist was excruciating and by the time I'd reached the dock, I was shivering and trembling with shock. Mum and the coach rushed over but, after examining my hand, they both came up with a different diagnosis. According to Mum, I needed an X-ray as well as a lie down. My coach decided that all I required was a couple of painkillers, some ice cubes, a bit of strapping and a quick pep talk. The latter consisted of telling me that if I didn't pull myself together and get back on the water, our team would lose the Team Title for the first time in twelve years. Mum was horrified but I understood how much was at stake and, albeit reluctantly and against my better judgement, did as he asked.

Slalom did not go well. As I turned towards buoys 2, 4 and 6, the pain was unbearable and it was simply impossible to give my usual standard. To add to my misery, Andy was furious and treated me with utter contempt. I tried to explain that my poor performance was due to the injury but he insisted it was a lame excuse. I walked away heartbroken at the angry words.

While slalom was better forgotten, tricks went surprisingly well. I think the fact that this discipline requires a different grip on the rope handle made it easier to achieve a good score.

When it came to jump, I was able to take most of the strain on my left hand and, with the agony reduced to tolerable levels, was once again able to give a satisfactory performance.

By the end of the tournament, Andy had what he wanted. The team had retained its title but as far as I was concerned, it was a hollow victory. The shock of the fire as well as my injury had taken its toll and all I wanted to do was go home. By the time we left Milan I couldn't even lift a cup of coffee with my right hand. Poor Mum, it certainly had been a memorable trip but for all the wrong reasons.

The day following our return, I went to see my sport physiotherapist who insisted I go immediately to hospital for an X-ray. Paul dropped me off at the local casualty department and when he rang a few hours later I told him I was starting the weekend in style. I was plastered!

Instead of the minor strain that Andy had diagnosed, I'd actually skied while suffering a broken wrist. I have to admit that ringing my coach to give him the news gave me no end of pleasure. I even threw in a bit of a lecture for good measure by reminding him that as I enjoyed a high pain threshold, any complaint on my part should be taken seriously. I think he learned his lesson and, with his sincere apology, our friendship survived.

The Recetto experience may have added a few grey threads to life's tapestry but, as I've discovered, there's always a beautiful contrast to run alongside. It didn't take long for me to recognise the highlight of the year when the then Deputy Mayor of Lisburn, Alderman Edwin Poots, rang to say that he was proposing I be awarded the Freedom of the City of Lisburn.

It's not like me to be lost for words but Edwin's announcement managed to stun me into silence. To be made a 'Freeman' is the biggest honour a city can bestow on one of its citizens and I was overcome with emotion. As well as pride and delight there was also enormous humility at such a privilege. When my voice returned, I asked Edwin the origins of the award and listened fascinated as he revealed how, in ancient times, a Freeman of the City was permitted to graze his sheep on any pasture he chose. Well, I don't have any mutton but maybe my woolly toy poodles would do instead.

With grazing at a premium in city streets, contemporary 'Freemen' are not required to own a flock of sheep. Instead, they become the ambassadors of their city as well as country. This was a role that, with my deep love of both, would prove no hardship to me. In fact, it was the perfect opportunity to give back a little of what I had been given.

The ceremony took place on Saturday 18 April. Family and friends flew in from Britain and further afield to join in the celebrations. With six of my cousins staying with us, our house was a hive of activity and excitement.

The proceedings started at 10 a.m. with Paul and myself being driven through the streets of Lisburn in a beautiful royal-blue open carriage, pulled by two large majestic black horses. People lined the route, cheering and clapping as we passed by; I had to compose myself on several occasions as I was almost overwhelmed with emotion and humility. I could hardly believe this was happening to me!

Lisburn City Council certainly knows how to do things in style. On our arrival at the Island Civic Centre, the red carpet was out! After the formal ceremony, I planted a rowan tree in the grounds. Then, Disability Sports NI along with children from one of the local primary schools entertained us with a demonstration of various paralympic sports.

A wine reception gave everyone a chance to mingle and walk through the fabulous exhibition which Eleanor Shields and her team had so artistically put together. Great attention was paid to detail, from the beautiful flower arrangements on the tables to the specially sourced material used for the covers of the programmes and menus. I was reliably informed that it looked like wet-suit material—and it certainly felt like it!

There were two hundred guests for the lunch, followed by speeches.

I was totally surprised when the Right Worshipful Mayor, Ronnie Crawford, invited me to unveil the Council's gift. It was a magnificent sculpture of me slalom skiing. The bronze was the fabulous work of the well-known sculptor John Sherlock. Although I had spoken with John earlier in the day, I had not given a second thought as to why he was at the conferring!

My sincerest thanks to Lisburn City Council. Blessed with sunshine, it was a perfect day, a truly magical experience— and one I will treasure for ever.

Epilogue

Whether it's Freeman of the City of Lisburn, Sports Personality of the Year, World Champion or any of the other umpteen illustrious titles I've managed to collect along the way, I think my favourite is still the simplest and perhaps most recognised: Janet Gray. The others may speak of honour and achievement but it is my name that denotes my identity. I am Janet, who, as a young girl, stumbled into a world of darkness. While I never returned to the sighted community, I pushed and fought my way back into its society. Not satisfied with remaining on the fringes, I decided to climb to the top, carving a niche in history and leaving others a trail of encouragement. My chosen tool was sport.

In 2004, on one of Florida's typical sunny days, fate knocked me from my summit of success into a cold and desolate valley where the only inhabitants were pain and despair. But, after assessing my choices, I decided that escape was better than self-pity or resigned acceptance and began the long laborious climb back to the top of the mountain. There was no magic potion or superhuman gene to ease the route. It was long, painful and incredibly difficult but I have inherited a limitless supply of stubborn determination that makes it impossible to quit.

Currently, as I work alongside Disability Sports Northern Ireland, my goal is to infuse others with the belief that every dream is possible. The importance of sport is impossible to value as it pushes the individual towards new horizons of personal and physical achievement. Regardless of disability, impairment, colour, creed or financial situation, sport is a playing field open to all.

My inspirational talks and seminars continue to introduce me to some wonderful people whom it has been a privilege to meet. Their stories never cease to enthral and encourage me and if, on occasion, my story offers hope or inspires a youngster to achieve his or her ambition, it will have been all worthwhile.

Water-skiing continues to be my passion. Yet, as life has shaped and honed me, I have discovered many new talents and other avenues that beckon with exciting possibilities. Undoubtedly, I will explore and sample the delights of media and speaking engagements. I do not know what the future holds or where it will lead. Nevertheless, I am certain that the journey of life is never without problems. The scent of roses permeates the air with the sweetest fragrance but nevertheless their thorns prick sore.

I have learned that it isn't the trial that matters. It could be major intrusions like my acquaintance with glaucoma, an unexpected introduction to a ski ramp that shattered bones as well as my life, or the awful pangs of bereavement and loss. It might simply be the frustrations of minor incidents such as a broken wrist or the 2009 theft of a favourite trick ski. Whatever the problem, there is only one solution. Do not give in; move on and find a way round the obstacle and focus on the more scenic aspects of the journey. For me, the touch of Paul's hand, my mum's voice, Pop's reassuring hug, Ian's cheerful banter and the generosity of friends like Mary Peters have provided even the bleakest landscape with a beautiful oasis.

Today, as the sun shines, warming my body, I sit on the dock, dangling my feet in the water, and wait. I am no longer the girl who tragically lost her sight. I am Janet, the woman who conquered all that fate had to throw and returned triumphant. I will never be the same, but then, who is immune from the footprint of time? Listening to the symphony of birdsong combined with the familiar note of

Paul's voice as he chats to friends on the boat, I am at peace and in love with life. In a moment or two, I will slip my feet into my ski, assume position and give the order that will send me swishing through the lake, spraying my face with tiny beads of water and filling my heart with excitement. It occurs to me that, like water-skiing, there is only one unmistakable command that will steer us through every situation in life. Prepared, ready to go, I shout it out, loud, confident and clear: 'Hit it!'

To book Janet to speak at your event
contact her on
www.janetgray.co.uk